I

Nigel Holmes has worked in the Anglican ministry in Jersey and Cambridge, and the surrounding area, for 30 years, having previously qualified in medicine. He is currently working in a freelance capacity in preaching and teaching, with a particular interest in the renewal and mission of the church today.

Looking for GOD

THE TRIANGLE POCKET LENT BOOK

NIGEL HOLMES

TRIANGLE

First published 1998
Triangle
SPCK
Holy Trinity Church
Marylebone Road
London
NW1 4DU

The publisher acknowledges with thanks permission to reproduce
the following publications:
Katherine A. M. Kelly, 'Give me a Sight, O Saviour', *Mission Praise*,
Marshall, Morgan and Scott © National Young Life Campaign, 1983.
Philip Larkin, 'Water', *The Whitsun Weddings* © Faber and Faber, 1964.
W. B. Yeats, 'The Second Coming', *The Collected Poems of W. B. Yeats*
© A. P. Watt Ltd/Faber and Faber, 1960.
11 lines from Philip Larkin, 'Church Going', *The Less Deceived*
© The Marvell Press, England and Australia, 1954.

British Library Cataloguing-in-Publication Data
A catalogue record for this book is available
from the British Library.

ISBN 0-281-05127-5

Typeset by Pioneer Associates, Perthshire
Printed and bound in Great Britain by
Caledonian International, Glasgow

Contents

For Anne and the family

Introduction

THE AIM OF THIS LITTLE BOOK is to help people look for God, and recognize him at the heart of everything, in a time when even the centre-stage of world affairs has no room to recognize his presence. However, once we learn how to look, we soon find ways in which God is very much at the centre of everything – which is not surprising, since he has created everything, and he upholds it every moment.

I have the idea that looking for God is like waiting for someone important coming to our house. We look out of the front door, for that is where important people come. If our expectations are not met, we turn away, concluding that he will not come this time. We get on with our business, and then for some reason, we open the back door – and to our surprise we find that God had left his answer there some time ago, while we were busy looking for him at the front door of our lives. On the grand scale, this too has been true. God began his 'great rescue operation' with Abraham and Sarah, a couple with no permanent home or established position, living on the edge of Canaanite society. He promised them a son, but this only came true when all normal expectations had failed. God took the people who lived at Egypt's back door, the slave community of Israel, and led them back to Canaan. Jesus arrived at the back door, in the stable at Bethlehem. He lived and taught in Galilee, only arriving in Jerusalem, on a donkey, in time for his

1

arrest and crucifixion. He died outside the city wall. He rose again, not for all the world to see, but in secret, to the amazement of his largely unbelieving followers.

Interfaces

In this space between the back door and the front door is our home, our life. We live in the interface between a busy world of expected events, and an unpredictable world of mysterious processes. Interfaces can take many forms. They can be physical, as for example the interface that exists between earth, air and sky at the sea-shore, where all sorts of things are going on, and where some of this book's themes find their starting-point. And they can be metaphorical, and can take the form of pictures. Jesus used such pictures in his parables. His parables brought people close to the interface where the mind, body and spirit interact, asking new questions, seeing new truths, choosing new pathways for further development.

I have now learnt to expect new thoughts about God, new insights from the Bible, to grow out of such back-door situations, partly those connected, say, with the disappointment of my current expectations (remembering that 'Our disappointments are God's appointments'); but also in what people nowadays call the serendipity of happening on a bright surprise. I am a beachcomber at heart, and have wasted many hours drifting along picking up junk, whether on the beach, from the skip, or on the television – to find the occasional object of real value, or simply to set me thinking. (My wife, Anne, may complain about the junk, but has always managed to find what she needs for science experiments with her infant class!)

One of my earliest memories is picking up spent bullets at an army range, my father being chaplain to a camp in the Rift Valley at the time. I even came home with an unexploded mortar, to everyone's consternation. An officer who was visiting the house dropped it down a very deep latrine. Time-wasting all this may be, but it goes with a desire to use my imagination – a trend which has been increased by people pressing me to make my sermons more interesting! I take heart, too, from what the great scientist Newton is supposed to have said: 'I do not know what I may appear to the world; but to myself I seem to have been only like a boy playing on the sea-shore, and diverting myself in now and then finding a smoother pebble or a prettier shell than ordinary, whilst the great ocean of truth lay all undiscovered before me.'[1]

Dawn is another interface, between night and day, and often stirs our imagination. I still remember dawn in the Channel Islands in the days when we worked for St Paul's Church in Jersey. Very early morning would sometimes see me up on the north cliffs, watching the sun rise over the distant shore of France. In a moment the pallor of dawn would be transformed into brilliant daylight, and a golden river would be unrolled across the sea, gilding every rock and islet, and igniting the cliffs and wooded valleys with glory. It brought home in a special way the idea that 'God's love covers over a multitude of sins' (1 Peter 4.8), which has become an important truth to me, in working for greater unity between people.

More recently, Anne and I visited Ulva, the beautiful rugged little island off Mull, just north of Iona. Rising out of a fjord-like loch, its crags are alive with falcon, eagle and sea birds. We learnt that David Livingstone's forebears lived on this tiny island – in a cave. The 'father of Australia', Lachlan MacQuarry, also came from Ulva, and his mausoleum stands at Gruline looking out over the waters of the loch. Such people grew up at the meeting-point of elemental processes, and no doubt it gave them a sense of awe, and taught them secrets of vision and initiative. On Easter afternoon when we were there, people of all denominations crossed in the little ferry for the annual united service in the chapel built by Thomas Telford. While the minister spoke from the upper storey of the three-tier pulpit, his sheepdog was sent out to nose his way among us in the congregation, to illustrate aspects of the sermon! Such places and occasions can leave a deep impression, and bring to life that interface where God's Spirit can work in us. They make us more imaginative, better able to help others 'see' God in ways that can bring his Word to life.

The Japanese theologian, Kosuke Koyama, who works at the interface between Christianity and Buddhism, has important things to say about how God can be recognized at the centre of everything. As David Ford says about Koyama's work: 'A central image is of "the broken Christ healing the broken world" not by ruling from the center but by going to the periphery . . .'[2] He uses this approach to explore the idea of idolatry, which he sees as the fundamental problem in our world. Idolatry takes over the centre by diverting its attention away from the challenge of ethical principles, commandeering all agendas to serve selfish ends. Idolatry rejects the need for ultimate meaning, and replaces it with the drive for instant efficiency, using modern technology to do the job, no matter what the longer-term consequences, and justifies itself on the principle that 'might is right'. The idol is a god which does not criticize its worshippers, but encourages them to save themselves, not others. Koyama's conclusion is that 'it is the crucified Christ who exposes the subtle essence and manifestation of idolatry.'[3]

We, too, have gone to the periphery, in a sense, like Jesus did with his parables, to create that interface where the human spirit deals with God. If, as a result, people can see God more clearly, know him more truly and love him more wholeheartedly, such blessings will not be kept at the periphery, far from the trampled streets of the metropolis, but have their power directed to the pressures, problems and opportunities of the city and the throng, and wherever else the need may be. Wisdom found on the periphery, in the wilderness, needs to become wisdom devoted to the transformation of the world, seen in the light of a clearer vision of the Kingdom of God.

The wilderness, for better or worse, seems to have got into my blood. We have lived in Cambridge for some years, and have found a nearby wilderness in the shape of the great estuary of the Wash, and have begun to discover the intimacies of the north-west corner of Norfolk. We can all go through life with our eyes and ears open to find those places, which like the wilderness, can be the interface where body, mind and spirit can engage with some of the mysteries which can fire our imagination, and help us see God in ways that bring our world and his Word to life.

1

Nisi Dominus

————————

AS OFTEN AS WE CAN these days, we live in our bungalow by Snettisham beach, which is four miles south of Hunstanton, in West Norfolk. The countryside was owned by the Le Strange family for centuries.[1] Their ancestor was granted rights by King John to control as much of the Wash as a galloping horse could enclose between high tides. Before that, William the Conqueror had given the region to William Albini, who built a fortress at Castle Rising, where Queen Isabella (who featured in the film *Braveheart*) ended her days. And long before that, even before the Romans, the Iceni buried treasure in carrstone pits beneath the soil of Ken Hill.

South of Snettisham stretches the royal estate of Sandringham, and in the 1900s this beach was Queen Alexandra's personal retreat. She never forgot her childhood at Bernstoff (near Copenhagen). 'She liked to recall the days when she sat unknown and obscure . . . looking out towards the Baltic, which could be seen gleaming in the distance between the waving boughs of the old beeches.'[2] Here too she could gaze across the sea and on the far horizon see the low vestiges of other shores, enthralled by the glittering expanse of sand and water, the flocks of waders and wildfowl, and the air filled with the cries of oystercatcher, redshank, curlew. She had a bungalow built of the warm brown local carrstone, at the very edge of the tide, with an upended boat as a sheltered garden seat. She crowned the roof-ridge with an engraved board: 'NISI DOMINUS A.R.I. A.E.D. MCMVIII'. 'Nisi Dominus' is how Psalm 127 begins, 'Unless the Lord builds the house, its builders labour in vain.' The following letters tell us: 'Alexandra, Queen and Empress, built 1908'. For seventeen years, the bungalow watched over the sands and shingles of Snettisham Scalp and Shepherd's Port. This cottage seems to have caught people's imagination. Postcards of it were popular. In 1909 a Leytonstone confectioner modelled the bungalow in a cake. It weighed 1600 lbs, was 4.5 feet high, 5.5 feet long and 2 feet wide. He used 1800 eggs, with fruit and flour.[3]

In those days, the gentle sweep of the Scalp was sweet green with soft grass. Shepherd's Port and Heacham Harbour formed a network of waterways behind the bar. Cockle gatherers would be out on the wet sands early in the morning gathering heaps of shellfish, the most famous being Hoddy Middleton and his daughter Elizabeth. They would then set off inland with their donkey and cart, covering a wide area, hawking the shell-fish and selling samphire in season. During the Christmas period of 1910 Queen Alexandra sent a hamper and two guineas to Robert (Peeps) Meek, who for many years dwelt alone in a hut on the beach.

Since then, a lot of the shingle on the beach has been quarried. Holiday parks have sprung up. Cockles have been 'hoovered away' by modern technology – so the numbers of oystercatchers have decreased. However, other species flourish, feeding on the lugworms and a rich menu of other nutrients. To the north is a Coastal

Park, towards the village a Common, and to the south a
bird sanctuary, while the line of quarry pits have become
lagoons. Gulls, terns, avocets, ring plover, skylarks breed
noisily in summer. In winter, waders, divers and ducks
abound, often filling the sky with whirling clouds of
shimmering wings, and fifteen thousand (and sometimes
twice as many) pinkfoot geese give a spectacular display
at the beginning and ending of each day. Skein after
skein fly over, not so much honking as yapping like
packs of eager puppies.

'Nisi Dominus' has not stood sentinel over the beach
for many years. When Alexandra died, George V had the
house demolished. However, the thought embodied in
the text she chose is as contemporary as ever and draws
our attention to the interplay between spiritual and
material reality.

God as the centre

The way we see God in the world, and in ourselves, can
make all the difference to the outcome of our life. Like
Moses in the story of the burning bush, we are treading
on holy ground, often without realizing it. In this chapter, the thread that runs through it all can be summed
up as: 'Nisi Dominus . . . Unless the Lord builds the
house, its builders labour in vain . . . but seeing God at
the centre brings everything to life.' It matters little
where we begin our quest, so let us start down on the
beach. We will find this trail soon leads us to surprising
treasures.

Someone has put two beehives by the beach, behind
the shingle ridge, above the long pond. There is no sign
of life in them, but they look pleasing. They do not

qualify to be called an apiary, but that may come, if some passing summer swarm decides to take up residence. As a one-time bee-keeper (until my wife Anne got too busy to look after them!) I think the bee world provides us with a striking parable.

One of the marvels of their world is its leadership. The Roman poet Virgil composed poems on rural life and agriculture. About bee-keeping, he wrote:

> While the king is safe, one faith is shared by all;
> But if he goes missing, their unity disintegrates;
> They destroy the golden hoard themselves
> And tear up the honeycombs.
> He safeguards their achievements;
> They worship him.[4]

Once, when we lived near Newmarket, one of our garden hives became increasingly ill-tempered. I moved it to Wood Ditton, whose woods guard one end of a Saxon earthwork ('Devil's Dike'), which runs from the forests to the fens. But then my 'bee king went missing' (the 'king', as we all know, is a 'queen'). When I brought them a new queen, I could see the bees – a hazy cloud harrying a poor lapwing which was flapping forlornly nearby. When I opened the hive, they turned on me. I was well protected, but later counted some two hundred stings in my green felt hat, which filled the gap above my veil. All the same, their new queen must have been well received as in a few days she had them calm and prosperous once more. Nowadays we know that bee society is held together by minute amounts of chemical (or pheromone), which the queen passes to her aides, who distribute it until the whole colony is covered or 'clothed', and all flourish.

Solomon, too, had studied agriculture. The Book of Proverbs is attributed to him, and he warns people that if they find honey, they ought to eat it carefully, as too much would upset them! (Proverbs 25.16). He also applied his wisdom to our spiritual needs. Perhaps Virgil knew more about bees, but Solomon knew that human beings also need a focal point of worship and that focal point is God. Without God at the centre of a nation's life, society disintegrates, for 'Where there is no revelation, the people cast off restraint' (Proverbs 29.18). The Hebrew words indicate that when priests and prophets fail to find fresh light from God, the people at large 'go unclothed' or unadorned.

When Solomon built the Temple, it was to be Israel's continuing focus for spiritual renewal. Priests and prophets were called to open their minds to God, and pass on the true meaning of justice, truth and wonder to the nation. But if they lost their inspiration, their vision would fail and their prophetic ministry would have to accommodate itself to the latest trends or to some king's personal ambitions, and then trouble would come, and the people would begin to feel frustrated, cynical, reckless – and unadorned.

Solomon's Temple was planned and paid for by his father, David. When he became king, after Saul and Jonathan had been defeated by the Philistines, he realized that the secret of success was to have God at the centre of everything. So, as he shouldered responsibility for a troubled and besieged nation, he did two things: first, he led a daring raid on a Jebusite city, which won him the possession of Jerusalem ('City of Peace'), to be his capital, and a strategic centre from which he could rally his new but disintegrating kingdom. And then, at the heart of Jerusalem, as the focus of national and spiritual vitality, he cleared a site for a house where God might set his name, and make his presence known. God was pleased, and promised David an everlasting kingdom. However, because David had been a 'man of war', God would not allow him to build the temple. Solomon (whose name means 'peaceful') was God's choice to do the work. What really mattered was not who financed it, planned it or managed the actual construction, but 'Nisi Dominus – Unless the Lord builds the house': God himself must be at the centre of all that is happening. Kings, priests, prophets and people had to constantly seek him, learn his ways and follow his commands. In that way, God's desire to bless them abundantly would be wonderfully realized year after year.

The importance of this principle was highlighted many times in the centuries that followed, as God's living presence continued to be marginalized by the selfish interests of the temple-keepers and succeeding kings. The supreme right of the Lord, their Divine King, to be at the centre of their life was usurped by various disastrous alternatives. Even in Solomon's time, the rot set in, as he began to add the gods of his foreign wives to the religious culture that developed in the temple. Later, Jeremiah poured scorn on a nation which trusted that the 'Temple of the Lord' would somehow guarantee their right to permanent survival, no matter how far they might fall spiritually from the true faith which the Lord demands. The 'builders', so busy in their endless political manoeuverings, were all labouring in vain – the outcome, as God had warned them, was judgement, national destruction, and exile.

By the time of Jesus Christ, the Temple (rebuilt by

Zerubbabel, and again by Herod) was once more failing
to be the vital spiritual centre the nation so urgently
required. When Jesus drove out the animals and over-
turned the tables of the money-changers, he declared: 'It
is written, "my house is a house of prayer for all nations,
but you have made it a den of robbers"' (Mark 11.17).
As a result, because the people were no longer sensitive
to the presence of God, they failed to recognize his hand
at work in Jesus' life and teaching, although Jesus had
visited the temple and taught in Jerusalem many times.

Jesus understood the inevitable consequences, and was
deeply moved by the tragedy he could foresee:

> As he approached Jerusalem and saw the city, he wept
> over it and said 'If you, even you, had only known on
> this day what would bring you peace – but now it is
> hidden from your eyes. The days will come upon you
> when your enemies will . . . encircle you and hem
> you in on every side . . . they will not leave one stone
> on another, because you did not recognize the time
> of God's coming to you.'
>
> (Luke 19.41ff)

If they had only known what was happening before
their eyes, how different the outcome would have been!
He would have drawn them together, renewed their
outlook and rebuilt their nation's life. Instead, he could
only lament what might have been:

> O Jerusalem, Jerusalem, you who kill the prophets
> and stone those sent to you, how often I have longed
> to gather your children together, as a hen gathers her
> chicks under her wings, but you were not willing.
> Look, your house is left to you desolate. For I tell

you, you will not see me again until you say, 'Blessed
is he who comes in the name of the Lord.'

(Matthew 23.37–39)

So we see that the history of Israel illustrates again and
again how vital it is to have nothing less than God, the
Living God, at the centre of life. No substitute will do
for 'Nisi Dominus – Unless the Lord . . .'! This truth is
still as relevant today. W. B. Yeats, from the turbulent
background of Ireland, chillingly describes the dynamics
of what is unleashed when moral decay collapses into a
spiritual vacuum, and opens the way for the 'coming' of
the vicious and ever-alert forces of anarchy:

> Turning and turning in the widening gyre,
> The falcon cannot hear the falconer;
> Things fall apart; the centre cannot hold;
> Mere anarchy is loosed upon the world,
> The blood-dimmed tide is loosed, and everywhere
> The ceremony of innocence is drowned;
> The best lack all conviction, while the worst
> Are full of passionate intensity.[5]

Even today, the principle of 'Nisi Dominus – Unless
the Lord . . .' confronts our busy lives with its challenge
and its promise. Traditionally, human society has focused
its religious activity on a place of worship, a house of
prayer. In Snettisham, St Mary's church stands above the
village. Its morning shadow falls over the village, which
looks up to see the spire catch the sun. It is a famous
landmark, its glorious west window faces the magnificent Wash sunsets which highlight the corresponding
'Stump' of Boston Church on the far side of the sea in
Lincolnshire. With St Mary's, the churches of Hunstanton,

Heacham, Ingoldisthorpe, Wolferton, Dersingham, Sandringham, and the little ruin at Babingley are strung out along the coast, breaking up the woods which clothe a gentle ridge of Norfolk carrstone, traditionally called the 'Christian hills', since it was here in the seventh century that St Felix first arrived to evangelize the Anglo-Saxons. Each church was built to be that vital community ingredient, a house of prayer for all the people, marking a turning-point in the achievement of those who had laboured for several previous centuries to build up the Christian faith among the people. Legend has it that Felix was shipwrecked near Babingley Creek, where he received invaluable help from a beaver, and decided to ordain him as a bishop on the spot! The village sign shows Felix and his ship; underneath, two beavers glide towards each other; while on top, bishop beaver, with crozier and mitre, blesses beaver number four.

Prayer and worship are the lungs of spiritual life. In the body the lungs and circulation provide another vivid parable of life with God at the centre. Some years ago, when I was a medical student, I remember a young woman who came to a surgical clinic at Papworth Hospital for a post-operative check. 'Tell us how you feel,' said the surgeon. '150 per cent,' she replied. 'What do you mean?' he asked. 'I used to think I was normal, 100 per cent,' she answered. 'But then I went in for a routine chest X-ray, and to my great surprise, they called me back. My heart was enlarged; I had a septal defect, a hole in the heart. Now it has been repaired, and I know what being normal really is; and I feel 150 per cent!'

A hole in the heart creates a short-cut for the blood. It can bypass the lungs and all those tiny capillaries. In some ways, it makes things easier! But the real effects are serious. Poisons like carbon dioxide are recirculated when they should be expelled, and the vital supply of oxygen is reduced. In a severe case, the result may be a 'blue' baby, but even in this young woman's milder case, an enlarged heart will lead to heart failure in later life.

Spiritual life can be hard work! To many, it seems easier to avoid it. But the consequences are serious. The poisons of life are recirculated, and build up within us. Bitterness, recrimination and unresolved feelings of guilt turn life blue at the edges. We also lose touch with the vital oxygen of God's grace, spiritual truth and divine love. It is 'those who wait on the Lord' who 'renew their strength'; who 'shall run and not be weary . . . walk and not faint' (Isaiah 40.31). But for others, there so often comes instead 'a famine . . . not of food, or a thirst for water, but a famine of hearing the words of the Lord' (Amos 8.11).

Because we all tend to adopt the conventional wisdom of our society as we grow up, we accept its cultural expectations as the norm. Living that way is what we would think of as 'feeling 100 per cent'. It may come as a shock to discover that there is a '150 per cent experience', and that God's loving plan for us is that nothing less should be our normal way of life. However, without his grace, 'normal life' remains impossible; but God's grace is near at hand, and as Jesus said, he had 'come that [you] might have life, and have it to the full' (John 10.10).

God's truth is the oxygen which fires our imagination and gives heart to our faith. We need prayer, as much as we all need air. And we need houses of prayer to bring us together, and feed the vitality of our community. We

also know that all these human institutions can lose
their vitality. So how can we recognize where God is at
work, and what can we do about it, if his presence seems
to be diminished? If we look through the Bible, we can
see how God's power and the recognition of his presence
can be restored.

God's power and presence

God's presence is connected with light, and the Bible
speaks of this as 'glory'. In early days, God revealed his
presence in this way on certain unique occasions, such
as by the light which shone over Mount Sinai on the
second occasion that Moses went up to meet with God:
'When Moses went up on the mountain, the cloud
covered it, and the glory of the Lord settled on Mount
Sinai . . . To the Israelites the glory of the Lord looked
like a consuming fire on top of the mountain' (Exodus
24.15–18).

A similar light filled the tabernacle once it had been
completed (Exodus 40.34), and similar radiance was
even reflected in people. When Moses descended from
Sinai with the Ten Commandments, his face shone so
brightly that the Israelites begged him to wear a veil till
it faded: 'When Moses came down from Mount Sinai
with the two tablets of the Testimony in his hands, he
was not aware that his face was radiant because he had
spoken with the Lord. When Aaron and all the Israelites
saw Moses, his face was radiant, and they were afraid to
come near him' (Exodus 34.29–30).

Such glorious happenings, however, were rare. Could
God's presence, with or without any outward manifestation, become part of the Israelites' daily life? Yes – once

seen, it could be sought continuously, through faithful prayer – and prayer symbolically integrated into the ceremonial of the nation's life. This was to be the next step in their 'learning curve', using olive oil, which came to represent the glory of the presence of God. Psalm 104 tells us that God not only gives us 'wine that gladdens our hearts, and bread that gives us strength', but 'oil that makes our faces shine'. Oil became a powerful religious symbol, and anointing became an important part of the consecration of a High Priest, and the coronation of a king. Anointing someone was an 'acted prayer', similar to: 'Lord, we anoint this Priest, this King, to make their faces shine, and so, O Lord, may you fill their lives and make them shine with your presence, your wisdom and your power.' The anointing of the High Priest became a vivid picture of the blessings that would be poured out upon the nation, as God's truth and power were focused and channelled from the centre of the nation's life to all its parts, just as the queen in the beehive spreads the evidence of her presence throughout the hive. It would bring about a precious and delightful unity: 'How good and pleasant it is when brothers live together in unity! It is like precious oil poured on the head . . . For there, the Lord bestows his blessing, even life for evermore' (Psalm 133).

However, oil was still only a symbol, of which the Holy Spirit is the reality. And so Isaiah moved the story on and turned the picture round. He envisaged not a priest or a king, but a great prophet, anointed not with outward oil but, inwardly, with the Holy Spirit: 'The Spirit of the Sovereign Lord is on me, because the Lord has anointed me to preach good news to the poor. He has sent me to bind up the broken hearted, to proclaim

freedom for the captives' (Isaiah 61.1ff). As a result, the
hope grew that one day a supreme Saviour, a Messiah,
would be raised up by God.

Messiah (the word for 'Christ', in Greek) means:
'Anointed One' – a Spirit-filled figure who would com-
bine the roles of prophet, priest and king, would bring
deliverance to Israel, inaugurate the Kingdom of God
and herald the New Age. And it was this text Jesus chose
to preach on at Nazareth, saying: 'Today this scripture is
fulfilled in your hearing' (Luke 4.17ff). Everything about
Jesus shone with the divine light of God's spiritual
presence, clearly visible to those who had eyes inspired
to see it. Outwardly, he looked like other people. He
had no 'halo'. The light that shone from him was of the
sort Isaiah spoke about, not a physical but a spiritual
'brightness'. There was one exception to this, the transfiguration, when Jesus appeared shining with physical
brightness to Peter, James and John: 'He was transfigured
before them. His face shone like the sun, and his clothes
became as white as the light' (Matthew 17.1ff). This
event confirmed Jesus as the Christ, but only to those
who had already 'seen the light', and confessed that Jesus
'was the Christ', the Son of God in the preceding
chapter (Matthew 16.16).

John's Gospel omits this dramatic story altogether.
His Gospel places more emphasis on the glory of God.
From the start, he proclaims that: 'We have seen his
glory, the glory of the one and only Son, who came from
the Father, full of grace and truth' (John 1.14); and he
makes this theme central to his purpose, in Chapter 12.
It seems as if John is saying: The transfiguration confirmed our belief that Jesus was the Messiah, but now it
is far more important to see what it means to be the

Messiah, the Anointed One. So, forget the 'halo', forget the transfiguration! I want you to see where that glory really does shine out – in a way that changes our understanding of God, and of everything else in heaven and earth. The light of the transfiguration tells us that God is in Jesus, but the glory that shines from the cross is a supreme revelation. It tells us that Jesus is God's unutterably precious and costly gift of love held out to every one of us, to redeem us at his own expense, and to save us for a life which is inspired by a just and holy love that reaches out far beyond anything we can imagine or desire.

Understood in this way, the progression of the idea is deeply moving. In fact, in the light of the cross, we can go back to the transfiguration and see it, too, in 'a new light', not just the light of the glory of God's omnipotence, but as the glory now made known to us in the vulnerable form of Jesus, and therefore, as unconditional love, shining right through to light up even the innermost recesses of the secrets of our hearts. This light is not something which God shines down onto everything, making it radiant and beautiful. Rather, God's light glows gloriously from and within the very heart of all he has created. When we accept Christ as our light, we find that this illuminates something within us which is like a flame of self-recognition.

The contrast between God's glory as external or internal to reality is well illustrated in a passage from the book *Jesus, Man of Prayer*, by Sister Margaret Magdalene. In a chapter on the glory of God, she tells how Metropolitan Anthony Bloom, the Russian Orthodox spiritual leader, drew her attention to two icons in the Tetriakov Gallery in Moscow. One is by Rublev, the other by Theophan the Greek:

The difference between the two icons lies in the way in which things are seen: the Rublev icon shows Christ in the brilliancy of his dazzling white robes which cast light on everything around. The light falls on the disciples, on the mountains, the stones, on every blade of grass. Within the light, which is the divine splendour – the divine glory, the light itself inseparable from God – all things acquire an intensity of being which they could not have otherwise, in it they attain a fullness of reality which they can have only in God. The other icon is more difficult to perceive in reproduction. The background is silvery and appears grey. The robes of Christ are silvery, with blue shadows and the rays of light falling around are white, silvery and blue. Everything gives an impression of much less intensity... One has the impression that these rays of divine light touch things and sink into them, penetrating them, touch something within them so that from the core of these things, of all things created, the same light reflects and shines back, as the divine light quickens the capabilities, the potentialities of all things and makes all reach out towards itself.

Looked at in this way, the transfigured Jesus shows that when God is at the centre of everything, 'all things acquire an intensity of being . . . attain a fulness of reality'; or perhaps, 'the divine light quickens the potentialities of all things and makes all reach out towards itself'.[6]

R.A. Finlayson, in a dictionary article on God, expresses the same truth in more theological terms:

God is Infinite Spirit, without bounds or limits to His being or to any of His attributes, and every aspect and element of His nature is infinite . . . In relation to the universe it implies both transcendence and immanence. By the transcendence of God we mean His detachment from all His creatures as an independent, self-existing being. He is not shut in by nature, but infinitely exalted above it . . . By the immanence of God we mean His all-pervading presence and power within His creation. He does not stand apart from the world, a mere spectator of the works of His hands: He pervades everything organic and inorganic, acting from within outwards, from the centre of every atom and from the innermost springs of thought and life and feeling, a continuous sequence of cause and effect . . . He is the eternal 'I am', and His present is eternity . . . It is not so much that God is everywhere; He is Himself the Everywhere . . . Holiness may be said to be . . . the outshining of all that God is.[7]

The dawn people

We can also retrace our steps from the cross and see how, for Jesus, 'Messiah' was an inclusive title. His people would share his glory and actively participate in his being. Compare his 'I am the light of the world' (John 8.12) with his: 'You are the light of the world' (Matthew 5.14). The kingdom of God has an anticipatory character: it lives in the present, but exists in the light of the future. It dawned with his arrival. It was triumphantly established on the cross and through the Resurrection. It received a powerful foretaste of the future through the outpouring of the Holy Spirit. But even with all this, the Kingdom of God has still not arrived in all its fullness. Until Christ returns 'upon the clouds

of heaven', the life of faith remains a great adventure,
where the promise of the future, like the dawn before
the sunrise, brings the world to life around us – but we
still await the coming of the sun.

In this way, then, the 'body of Christ', the Holy Spirit
community, has to be a people of the 'dawn', and what
could be more evocative than that? Nothing stirs the
senses as vividly as a summer dawn under a clear sky.
Sunrise is wonderful, but the earlier moments have a
very special quality. Let this idea of dawn stir our imagination! For instance, picture the Norfolk first light, as
one who looks out from the hills above the River Burn,
over Burnham Market, across misty marshes and the
saltings, to the grey North Sea. It has a silver sheen. Land
air and sea are still folded together, stirring dove-like to
meet another day. We know the sun is coming, but as yet
it remains hidden, only hinted at by a limpid brightness
on the far horizon. No doubt, Nelson, raised in the
vicarage at Burnham Thorpe, would have walked that
hill, marking time as it were, for five long years when he
came home on half-pay (or as we might say nowadays:
'was unemployed'). He was someone who had already
learnt how to use his frustration, even pain, to help
focus his life more clearly. As one of England's greatest
leaders, he was greatly admired by all the rank-and-file
he commanded. Like all true leaders, he had to perfect
his ability the hard way. Rather than let this period go
to waste, he allowed it to mature his genius. He continued to believe his day would come.

Jesus, too, shows that the patience demanded of
'dawn' people is fundamental to God's own way of
doing things: 'In bringing many sons to glory it was fit-
ting that God, for whom and through whom everything

exists, should make the author of their salvation perfect through suffering . . . Jesus is not ashamed to call them brothers' (Hebrews 2.10–11). Being a 'dawn' person is hard going, but it works! 'Weeping may remain for a night, but rejoicing comes in the morning' (Psalm 30.5). This is because, as Gerard Manley Hopkins put it in 'God's Grandeur', the Spirit of God is constantly at work enveloping every present darkness with the freshness of the a new day dawning:

> Nature is never spent;
> There lives the dearest freshness deep down things;
> And though the last lights off the black West went
> Oh, morning, at the brown brink eastward, springs –
> Because the Holy Ghost over the bent
> World broods with warm breast and with ah!
> bright wings.[8]

Another special place where dawn illustrates these truths for me is Zermatt, the Swiss Alpine resort, which finds shelter in a little valley, but is constantly aware of the Matterhorn's fearful, graceful, beauty towering above it. In the valley, darkness comes early and stays late. But long before the sun's rays reach down to warm the shops and chalets, they touch the great peak and turn it into a resplendent beacon. In the little graveyard of St Peter's (English) church, one family has set a memorial for their son, one of many who died climbing the Matterhorn. They have taken a phrase by Shakespeare's Romeo, and have inscribed this epitaph: 'Jocund day stands tip-toe upon the misty mountain top' – which is a brilliant touch: By choosing those words, they have transformed the pinnacle that towers above the grave from being the cruel symbol of a tragedy into the glorious representation of a greater hope. We too can bring the same perspective of hope to bear on the darkest shadows of our life. As the old hymn puts it:

> And lo! Already on the hills,
> The flags of dawn appear.
> Lift up your heads, ye prophet souls,
> Proclaim the Day is near.[9]

However, so long as we live in the present age, good and evil will continue to oppose each other. Like the tides, the battle will flow this way and that. The Bible talks about evil 'coming in like a flood', but God will raise up a standard against it. The next chapter looks at this battle, and our progress in it. It goes on to examine how God supports us in the battle, and how this is particularly represented in baptism, and the picture of the tides and floods.

In the meantime, nothing remains of Queen Alexandra's bungalow. The carrstone went to Shernborne to help build an attractive village hall, and now only a few foundation fragments can still be seen after a more severe storm than usual has scoured the beach. However, the spirit in which it was built still challenges us with its warning, 'Nisi Dominus – Unless the Lord builds the house, its builders labour in vain . . .', and calls us to reach out to the Living God, who in return promises to bring the whole of our world to life.

For further reflection

1. If you had been Queen Alexandra, aged 60, what would you have carved on the ridge over your beach bungalow? What do you think the

Psalmist meant by, 'Unless the Lord builds the house, its builders labour in vain. Unless the Lord watches over the city, the watchmen stand guard in vain. In vain you rise early and stay up late, toiling for food to eat – for he grants sleep to those he loves' (Psalm 127.1–2)?

2. The transfiguration (Matthew 17) follows Peter's confession that Jesus is Christ, or 'anointed one' (Matthew 16). What is the link? Why might John have left out the story of the transfiguration, in the light of John 12. 23–24?

3. Try this bio-feedback experiment! Find the pulse at your wrist, and put a finger on it. Count the beats in a minute. Hold your breath, and count another minute. Take deep breaths and count another minute. What do you feel about the way your heart and your lungs connect and influence each other? Do you feel healthy? Do you feel you need to take more exercise or eat better? Do you feel your whole self is well integrated? Do you feel your body, mind and spirit are operating as a temple of the Holy Spirit? Do you think you are experiencing 150 per cent life as the normal way you live? What lesson can you take from these feelings? What short prayer to God can you make which will express your response to these feelings?

4. In what ways, if any, do you think this chapter has helped you recognize God at the centre of everything?

2
Wash and flood

————— ◦●◦ —————

The force of water

THE LANDS AROUND THE WASH on the east coast of
England are the scene of a constant battle between earth
and water, with the waves and the sand, to and fro, an
interface which can stir our imagination to look for
God afresh. Daniel Defoe called this area the sink of
thirteen counties. The fens and marshlands hold out
against the Wash and its four rivers, the Witham, the
Nene, the Welland and the Great Ouse, and many
tributaries, like the Lark, the Wissey and the Old West
with their drainage channels, 40–Foot, 100–Foot and New
Cut. People exploit the wealth of the black soil, while
water works to win it back. Graham Swift's novel *Waterland* is the story of a teacher trying to interest bored fen
students in the French Revolution. He finds what really
stirs them is the grim, compelling and still unresolved
history which began years ago in his own family's life
down among the sluices and weirs of his father's lock.
The Wash becomes a metaphor of the mysterious
powers with which people have to contend as they
struggle to cope with life. In describing its unremitting
pressure, he says:

> The Wash summons the forces of the North Sea to its
> aid in a constant bid to recapture its former territory.

For the chief fact about the Fens is that they are reclaimed land, land that was once water, and which, even today, is not quite solid . . . You do not reclaim a land without difficulty and without ceaseless effort and vigilance . . . strictly speaking the Fens are never reclaimed, only being reclaimed.[1]

The Celts learnt to walk on stilts, and built stilt villages, remains of which were found at Flag Fen near Peterborough. The Romans built barriers, dug drains and cultivated the rich soil. Anglo-Saxons planted settlements, and became skilful fishermen and wildfowlers. Early Christians founded communities on small islets in the bogs ('ea's, like Manea and Stonea, and 'ey's like Whittlesey and Ramsey). A Life of St Guthlac (written soon after Guthlac's death in 715), presented a graphic scene:

There is in the midland district of Britain a most dismal fen of immense size, which begins at the banks of the river Granta not far from the town which is called Cambridge and stretches from the south as far north as the sea [i.e. The Wash]. It is a very long tract, now consisting of marshes, now of bogs, sometimes of black waters overhung by fog, sometimes studded with wooded islands and traversed by the windings of tortuous streams.[2]

Having trained for monastic life, Guthlac travelled to the Granta, where a local man named Tatwyne guided him in a fishing skiff through trackless bogs to the remote and desolate isle of Crowland. Here, beside an ancient burial mound, he made his dwelling. It was the year 699, and he was 26. Felix recounts the torments he suffered from the attacks of demonic forces, night after night, seeking to drive him from their dark domains. He felt surrounded by hideous faces, filthy beards, stinking breath, fiery mouths and echoing screams (perhaps fen fever, common in those days, contributed to his dismay) – but he won through. He was a gentle man, whose compassion drew others to him. His helpfulness and healing powers won him respect and fame. He also had an empathy with animals, and skill in taming them. It is said that swallows would even come to him for guidance in where to build their nests.[3]

The great change in the Wash began in the seventeenth century, with the draining of the fens under Cornelius Vermuyden, although the Ouse project exhausted his resources, leaving him a poor man. The fens were then above sea level, and Vermuyden, only aiming to provide summer pasture, drained the water by 'natural fall' – misunderstanding how such water flows, and sediment accumulates. The silt built up, and his scheme faltered. But other projects followed and steadily reclaimed the land against fierce opposition from the fenmen, whose way of life was severely curtailed. Once, the wildfowl would 'rise like thunder' if they were disturbed, but in time the fens stood largely silent. The shrinkage and erosion of the dry peat after drainage caused the land to sink below sea level. Horse-driven pumps had to be installed, then a myriad of windmills. Old dried-up river beds (or roddons), whose gravelly silts often now support rows of buildings, can be seen snaking across the landscape; while banked rivers may flow as much as twenty feet above such roads as run beside them.

In 1713 a torrent of tidal water smashed Denver Sluice, and it was 35 years before a new one was built. The 100-Foot, so vital to the south level, burst its banks in 1799, 1805, and 1809, drowning 6,000 acres on each occasion. A 'drown' became the word chosen by fenmen for these deluges – more appropriate than 'flood' or 'inundation'. After wind power came steam, and one engineer, waxing lyrical, inscribed a poem on the wall of the 100-Foot pumping station near Little Downham:

These fens oft-times have been by water drowned,
Science a remedy in water found,
Power of steam, she said, shall be employed,
And the destroyer by itself destroyed.

In May 1863 incoming tidal water rushed down the Marshland Cut, crashed through the sluice at Middle Level Drain, bursting its banks to flood 8,000 acres. 'Drowns' recurred in 1912, 1928, and 1937. In early March 1947, the waters made their supreme attack, aided by storm-force winds, on a countryside barely recovering from the Second World War. Throughout January and February Arctic weather had descended on Britain. Snow piled high, and even the sea froze. As one eye-witness put it: 'From the sea it was just as if it were in small wavelets and it had frozen, and we were walking on it in our Wellington boots; and even when the tide went down all this frozen sea still remained high. It were just one mass of ice.'[4]

Coal stocks had been run down, and electricity supplies were cut, but as street lights were turned off, the elemental beauty of the sea generated its own mysterious illumination. The grey North Sea can display amazing luminescence, and it is a unique experience to row out in pitch darkness from the Scalp and see the water light up with silver fire, flames leaping from the prow, while the oars return a cascade of molten light each time their blades are lifted. To dip one's cupped hand in and out is to see a score of brilliant diamonds glittering on one's inky palm. That same February, another witness experienced this luminescence vividly:

I was in a ship running from Harwich to Antwerp, a passenger boat called the *Accrington*. We were on a night crossing, and mostly the illumination was starlight; and this sheet ice had broken into huge slabs like crazy paving, and all the outline of the slabs was like a blue fire from the phosphorescence in the water. And it was quite eerie because it was flat, but it didn't go to the horizon, as there was a haze band and it vanished into this haze band which was a glowing band, it glowed with starlight, and above it came the stars and the heavens, really a most remarkable picture, quite beautiful. I always remember saying to a chap on the deck, 'It would make a lovely setting for a ballet dance.' It had a timeless feeling about it as though we were cocooned, as though we were away from the world we had known, and a dramatic silence. It wasn't oppressive, it was, how do you describe it? It was – you looked at it – it was a sense of wonderment; it was like something out of a fairy story, you know, you expected – the tales of your childhood – some ice princess to come floating down; but the total effect was beautiful.[5]

In March, a sudden thaw began. Water gushed into the fens from all directions. All hands were called out to strengthen the defences, even German prisoners-of-war played a part in bolstering the banks, whose traditional construction was said to resemble a mixture of compost and tooth-paste – peaty soil, layers of osier matting and dense clay. Large parts of East Anglia were submerged and farms were swept away. One farmer rowed his boat through his house, whose walls had burst apart.

January 1953 saw the coastal defences breached far and wide, and many people were drowned. Our little bungalow at Snettisham stood firm, but the one to the left was washed away, and that on the right up-ended. An even greater surge occurred in February 1978, sweeping the Hunstanton pier away. However, substantial defences were now in place, and largely held the sea at bay. The more the coast is defended, the more high tides are funnelled into King's Lynn, up the Ouse. The medieval church of St Margaret has a series of engraved metal plates on the arch of the west door, marking where various floods have flowed into the nave! Rubber-sealed barrage gates guard the town along the river front. Now, global warming is adding a new factor to the conflict: ocean waters rise – and Scandinavian glaciers melt, which reduces the weight on the crustal rocks. As they rise, East Anglia sinks a millimetre annually in compensation! The task of land reclamation is changing, too. Only ten years ago thought was being given to enclosing the Wash, but priorities have changed. As wildlife habitat is depleted, the priority is now to preserve our wetlands, even to return agricultural land to wilderness.

Tides and floods of faith

The human story also has its tides and floods. What strange forces wax and wane to influence the spiritual vagaries of human culture? In the conflict between good and evil, the outcome flows this way and that. Each new phase brings its gains and losses, advances and retreats. 'The signs of the times', as Jesus called them, leave their mark on the placid rural scene just as much as on the bustling metropolis. For instance, when we tried to reach the Peter Scott Coastal Walk in Wingland via a short-cut on our map, we found the way barred. The farm had suffered a series of incidents of theft, arson and vandalism – farmers nowadays have to cope with a rising tide of crime out of all proportion to any problems they had 30 years ago. Rural areas can be as affected by the problems of drug abuse as the towns, nor is Norfolk immune to social ills, family breakdown, hopelessness, and the polarizing gap between rich and poor.

Our culture, while no doubt in crisis, is not necessarily heading for catastrophe. The Japanese word for crisis is made up of two characters which mean 'danger' and 'opportunity'. Just as the crises caused by ever-rising waters have led to new initiatives and fresh resources, so human crises can be creative moments for those who see God at the centre of everything. The danger is that the community of faith can and, at present, has been marginalized. If we look at the churches, we may agree with those who deplore the fact that too many have become 'private zoos', where people withdraw to practise their devotions in a context which is largely alien to the world outside. There are, of course, many reasons for this. Scientific progress has shaken many of the old assumptions about life, and technology has made people feel so much in control of their existence that a religious outlook seems outmoded. Social mobility and the information revolution have led to greater awareness of other religious and philosophical traditions, giving rise to the impression that all truth is relative, so that pluralism should be accepted as the cultural norm. As a result, major social issues are dealt with from a secular perspective. Although this shift away from the traditional Christian view has taken effect throughout society in the twentieth century, it was in the nineteenth century that the implications were seen by those who could read the signs of the times. Matthew Arnold's poem 'Dover Beach' has often been used to illustrate this:

> The Sea of Faith
> Was once, too, at the full, and round earth's shore
> Lay like the folds of a bright girdle furled.
> But now I only hear
> Its melancholy, long, withdrawing roar,
> Retreating, to the breath
> Of the night-wind, down the vast edges drear
> And naked shingles of the world.
> . . . Ah, love, let us be true
> To one another! for the world, which seems
> To lie before us like a land of dreams,
> So various, so beautiful, so new,
> Hath really neither joy, nor love, nor light,
> Nor certitude, nor peace, nor help for pain;
> And we are here as on a darkling plain
> Swept with confused alarms of struggle and flight,
> Where ignorant armies clash by night.[6]

Can we read the signs of our times, and interpret them to the people of our age? The question of where today's trends point requires our attention and should rouse our sense of opportunity. At first sight, the situation seems complex. Conventional wisdom, based on 'modernism', which looked at life as if 'man is the measure of all things' is a movement in retreat. All that makes up the

strange phenomenon of 'post-modernism' is gaining
ground. Religious life and Church affairs struggle on,
but those with a simple faith feel that their beliefs are
being attacked from within (modern and post-modern
theology) and from without (relegation to the side-lines
by society at large). One could be excused for echoing
the despairing words of Mary Magdalen: 'They have
taken away my Lord, and I don't know where they have
put him!' (John 20.13). But once we recognize what is
really happening, we can interpret it to others. Many
people are being carried along by trends, absorbing their
underlying suppositions unwittingly, and letting these
trends condition their views on life.

Christians should be able to out-think, out-live and
out-love the rest of the world, because with faith in a
crucified Christ to sustain us, we can learn to face disaster with an unflinching gaze, believing that even to lose
everything is still worthwhile, because in the mysterious
purposes of a just and loving God, truth is to be valued
above all. This means we do not have to cling to, let
alone rest in, any other source of confidence we may
have inherited or developed. So, again and again, we can
let go of our defensiveness, our gratifications, our status
and popularity. Therefore, we can and should always be
learning to take the lead in the quest for truth, justice
and compassion. Christians must be those who can live
at the unstable interface between the incoming tides of
danger, on the one hand, and the dykes and sluices, the
compost and toothpaste defences, which hold the way
open, on the other hand, for opportunity and progress.

There are Christians who believe post-modernism
can be a fertile ground in which to present the faith.[7]
This has, at least in part, arisen out of a revulsion at the

oppressive power structures of modernity – and who
defined the ways of freedom more radically than Jesus?
So, while we may look at the prevailing scene, and feel
a lot must change before the ebbing tide of faith can
flow again, the outlook remains encouraging. Jesus had
a word for his followers that should stir us as much as it
did them: 'Do you not say: "four months more and then
the harvest"? I tell you, open your eyes and look at the
fields! They are ripe for harvest, even now' (John 4.35).

How, then, can we regain our nerve, reiterate the
truth of 'Nisi Dominus' and present the fact that God is
'at the centre' to a world in crisis? How are we to show
that this is a time of danger *and* opportunity? First, our
own faith must be rekindled. 'Faith comes from hearing
the message, and the message is heard through the word
of Christ', says St Paul (Romans 10.17). Sadly, many of
our religious concepts, practices and forms have become
standardized and stale. They no longer capture our
attention, fire our imagination, or bring our world to
life. But this is not the first time faith has run low, and
then the tide has turned. In John the Baptist's day, the
voice of prophecy had fallen silent; then he appeared,
with a message which captured the imagination of the
whole community. How did he turn the tide? He took
hold of an old truth whose presentation had become
outworn, and reclothed it with freshness and immediacy
– and he lived the way he preached. He was disturbing,
convincing and inspiring.

The truth he brought to life was their own ancient
story, but it had been fossilized. Like some Jurassic DNA,
the spiritual 'germ within the fossil' was still a potentially
revolutionary truth. God used John to reconstitute it,
clothe it in a contemporary form, and communicate it

in such a way as to prepare people for a new stage in that same story. Just as, long ago, the Israelites led by Joshua had stood before the River Jordan, poised to enter the long-sought-for promised land (Joshua 1), so now, a far greater promise was to be fulfilled: the Messiah's imminent arrival! But the nation was not fit for such a time. They had moved far from the light of God. They would never recognize the Anointed One, should he stand before them. Their selfish thoughts, their deceitful words, their anxious eyes and hardened hearts were unreceptive; while layers of hypocrisy had been accumulated – a process of decay which has recurred so often, and which Gerard Manley Hopkins immortalized in his poem 'God's Grandeur':

> Generations have trod, have trod, have trod;
> And all is seared with trade; bleared, smeared
>   with toil;
> And wears man's smudge and shares man's smell:
>   the soil
> Is bare now, nor can foot feel, being shod.[8]

John's baptism, 'a baptism of repentance', proclaimed it was high time to take the nation to God's laundry at the River Jordan! But the symbolism of water and the faithful preaching which accompanied it says so much more as well, if instead of letting our eyes wander over the mere surface of the river, we gaze into its depths. We can see death in the water, two great 'drownings', Noah's flood and Pharaoh's doom, first, when a wicked world was swept away under God's righteous judgement; and second, when Israel finally broken free from bondage to the Egyptian tyrant. We can see renewal, too, in Noah's dove with the olive branch, a new beginning, and a world ready to be born again. For Israel, we can see a nation finally emerging from forty years of pilgrimage, leaving an unbelieving generation buried in the past (still hankering for Egypt); while under Joshua's leadership, we see a new nation, setting off to claim the promised land.

We can see the healing stream, the Jordan, which the Syrian general Naaman at first glance despised, when told to wash in it to have his leprosy healed. But this is no ordinary river; it is a unique and noble torrent! It rises pristine from the living rock at Caesarea Philippi, fed by the snows of 10,000-foot-high Mount Hermon, plunging down to sea level, and then on 600 feet lower, to the Sea of Galilee, surrounded by its little towns and rugged hills. It goes on falling, along the line of the Great Rift Valley (which itself stretches 3,000 miles here from Africa), on and down to where John was baptizing, and on and down to Jericho, and finally to that 'world sump', the Dead Sea, 1200 feet below sea-level. There it disappears, vaporizing in the heat, leaving great mineral deposits which cover the ancient cities of Sodom and Gomorrah. Elisha the prophet told Naaman that his leprosy could be cured by washing in the Jordan. He initially refused, preferring his Syrian streams, Abana and Pharpar, rivers of Damascus (2 Kings 5). But no river on earth has Jordan's pedigree, its geophysical uniqueness, or its power to raise the human spirit; and it was in the Jordan and only in the Jordan that God ordained that this proud general should be made clean.

John, however, did not dwell on the past glories of the river. He spelt out the meaning of repentance for the perplexed citizens, vigilant men-at-arms and busy tax collectors of his day, as 'with many other words' he 'exhorted the people and preached the good news to them' (Luke 3.18). He blended forceful urgency with a striking humility; and the word he is associated with, 'baptize', is an energetic and a humbling one. This is seen in the way the word is spelt – a Greek word whose root is: 'bapt-'; so 'bapto' means 'I dip'. Adding '-iz-' intensifies it; so 'baptizo' means 'I dip strongly': 'I plunge, I fill, I flood – even I drown . . .'.

To bring the point home, I like to imagine two religious leaders, John the Baptist, and John the Bapter. The Bapter would have been busy, kindly and popular with those he met. He did not cut much ice, but he was nice. Although he disapproved of what Herod the tetrarch was up to with his brother's wife Herodias, and of the many other evils he had done, he only suggested it might lead to problems in the future. John the Bapter would have lived to sedate retirement, even in those dangerous days. But that fact is, we have never heard of John the Bapter, though surely there have been many like him. Such religious people seem more comfortable performing the obsequies of a dying faith, than turning up the brilliance of God's light anew.

John the Baptist, by contrast, believed that 'faith is spelt r.i.s.k.' While many gave him their allegiance (his following even spread after his death), he insisted in his humility he was 'not fit to undo the sandals' of the coming Christ; for, as he said, 'He must become greater; I must become less' (Luke 3.16 and John 3.30). In the meantime (Luke 3.19), John rebuked Herod Antipas for his unlawful marriage to Herodias, among other things. Herod had divorced his own wife to marry her. Herod had him arrested, and finally John was beheaded at the instigation of Herodias. Later, however, Aretas, father of

Herod's divorced wife, waged war on Herod, and many believed that Herod's heavy defeat was a divine retribution for the killing of John.

What can we learn from John? We must want to do as he did. Simply to accept the *status quo* and make the best of it is the way of a 'Bapter', not a 'Baptist'! Jesus called his followers 'the light of the world' and 'a city set on a hill, which cannot be hidden' (Matthew 5.14). We must turn up this light, come out of the 'private zoo' and build God's city out there in the open for all to see. We must make it our ambition to catch the attention of the whole community, fire its imagination and provoke its thirst for the living waters of spiritual reality.

The living waters of spiritual reality

Where better to start to search for the living waters of spiritual reality than in the church buildings which have become our zoo? What happens when we go to church? No doubt if you are a newcomer, it all seems strange these days. If you are an old hand, you simply settle down in your familiar groove. In either case, we are blind to what is really there! But God is here too, at the centre of everything, bringing the building wonderfully to life, if only we had the imaginative power to recognize his presence. Even an agnostic like Philip Larkin could recognize something significant in the silent message of a local church, because he used his imagination. His poem, 'Church Going', gives us a clue on how to 'see' beyond the limits familiarity imposes:

> Once I am sure there's nothing going on,
> I step inside, letting the door thud shut . . .

A serious house on serious earth it is,
In whose blent air all our compulsions meet,
Are recognized, and robed as destinies.
And that much never can be obsolete,
Since someone will for ever be surprising
A hunger in himself to be more serious.
And gravitating with it to this ground,
Which he once heard, was proper to grow wise in,
If only that so many dead lie round.[9]

Even before we enter the church building, we see in the
quiet graves of those beneath that 'serious earth' some
who, though asleep, are facing East, ready to spring to
life again on the Day of Resurrection. When we step
inside, we must focus our imagination in the right order
for the story all around us to unfold. Perhaps it is one
of those Sundays when the church is full of flowers –
forget them! They must not distract us at this stage from
the water. A great rushing torrent, which continually
fills the entry to the nave of every church! Why have we
lost sight of something so demanding in its symbolism?
Larkin again supplies us with a clue:

> If I were called in
> To construct a religion
> I should make use of water.
>
> Going to church
> Would entail a fording
> To dry, different clothes;
>
> The litany would employ
> Images of sousing,
> A furious devout drench.[10]

At St Mary's, Snettisham, the font stands at the entrance

to the church, under the beautiful West window which Seymour's *Companion Guide to East Anglia* calls 'the glory of the place ... Decorated at its most free and exciting ... lacework in stone'.[11] Forget the window: to bring the world to life we must focus on the font. Let the font be the window of our imagination. Font means fountain, and it represents the River Jordan. Now at last we can see it, a river flooding through the nave, threatening, inviting, liberating, inspiring! Each time we enter church, our hearts and minds should be lit up by the memory that we once crossed this river, and now live in the promised land, where heaven comes to Earth.

The church stretches itself out west to east, between this fountain and a feast. At this end, though baptism is a once-and-for-all event, we must always be ready to 'launch out into the deep' again, into the fullness of all God has for us. His grace and power are here to turn life upside down and inside out ... so pain becomes a path to blessing, problems become a prelude to discovery and 'disappointments become God's appointments'. Turning from here to the far end of the church, we set off to the feast, God's banquet, so simple to look at, but in Christ rich, satisfying and unfailing – the more we share of it, the more its riches grow.

Once we have learnt how to recognize the pictures that can be switched on in a church, so much of God's Word comes to life again. This is important, because it is his Word that ultimately washes us: 'Christ loved the Church and gave himself up for her to make her holy, cleansing her by the washing with water through the word, and to present her to himself as a radiant church, without spot or wrinkle or any other blemish, but holy and blameless' (Ephesians 5.25–27).

However, the truth of God's Word needs the power of God's Spirit; and John promised that while he baptized in water, Christ would baptize in the Holy Spirit. Like the luminescent waters of the sea, baptismal water symbolizes spiritual light and fire. Many of us start to be nervous when we see how deep God's water is. Rather than plunge into its fullness, which means letting go of what we are used to, and taking the risk of going against the stream, and perhaps ending up where we had never planned to be, we keep one foot firmly on the solid world we have grown up in, and cling to the handrail of convention. While we are rightly cautious about many things in life, we should not be so about our heavenly Father's love. Baptism commands us not merely to dip our toes in the river of God's life, but take our foot off the bottom, let go of the handrail, and learn how to swim in the full current of God's purpose for our lives. Let us, then, put the '-iz-' back into 'bapting', and the 'fizz' will find its way back into our faith's new wine! Jesus promised: 'Come to me and drink, and out of your hearts will flow rivers of living water' (John 7.37).

We cannot leave the subject of water without a brief mention of the amazing Margery Kempe of Lynn (1372–c. 1440). Famous for her weeping, and renowned for the way the flow of God's 'living water' filled every aspect of her life, she was the daughter of John Brunham, the city's mayor and MP, and married kind and supportive John Kempe, bearing fourteen children. With her first pregnancy she became very ill and depressed, and had to be manacled to prevent her from harming herself. Everything changed when she had a beautiful and calming experience, as Christ appeared to her, sat by her bedside, and asked why she had forsaken one who had never left her. The air seemed to blaze with light, and the vision ended. In that moment, she was well again. Full of a new energy, she began to engage in various business enterprises, became a leading brewer, and then ran a corn mill. She lived in style, paid her husband's debts, and sported the height of fashion – until everything began to go wrong. Convinced that God was saving her from a life of worldly vanity, she devoted herself to Christ, and became active at St Margaret's church. She studied avidly, by getting others to read to her as she was illiterate. She gave time to meditation, especially on the cross and suffering of Christ who had done so much to save her. She was visited by scholars and religious leaders, while actively running a household where everything had the touch of God's grace in it (when she cooked the stock fish and the skin stuck to her hands, it seemed Christ was commending her for holding fast to him through thick and thin). Her weeping when deeply moved (which was often!) was seen by some as a spiritual charism; but when it happened loudly in the sermon, angry members of the congregation would wish she were at sea in a boat with no bottom! She and her husband began to travel because she believed God gave her messages for the church at large. When her husband had a serious accident, she became his devoted nurse; and when he died, she continued her travels, by boat up the Ouse to help the Poor Clares at Denny Abbey, by foot across Norfolk to take advice from Julian of Norwich. To Canterbury, Lincoln, Bridlington, Bristol she went, then across the sea (which she disliked) to Rome, Assisi, Jerusalem, Spain and Germany.

Her faith was intense, visionary, often prophetic, and her prayers were powerfully effective in many lives. She was put on trial for being a Lollard (travelling preachers who followed the reformer John Wycliffe), but was acquitted. She was often quite critical of church dignitaries, even archbishops, on occasion, but usually these criticisms were accepted and acted on, as her sincerity and concern were so transparently humble and self-effacing. All this was bound up with a self-sacrificing concern for others of all sorts. When in Rome, she shared the hovel of a poor old woman, caring for her, begging for her in the street, cutting up sticks to make a fire to cook for her. In her youth, lepers had disgusted her, but through her discovery of God's love, her attitude changed, and she would readily embrace them, and do all she could to help them. Finally, she persuaded Master Robert Spryngold, vicar of St Margaret's, Lynn, to write her memoirs, which she dictated (*The Book of Margery Kempe*, 1436). It has become a classic of medieval literature, full of detail and colour, shining with spiritual life. Margery, then, is a historical example of someone in ordinary circumstances, who immersed herself in the love and life of God, and she wrote her book for ordinary people, 'to bring them comfort and solace, and to help them to understand the indescribable love and mercy of our sovereign saviour, Jesus Christ'.[12]

Perhaps a word of warning is required at this point. As we saw above, Word and Spirit must be held together, and individual inspiration must be subject to the Church under the authority of Scripture. Deep waters can encourage sharks – people who learn how easy it can be to manipulate others for their own advantage. We must be on guard, so as not to drift out of that mainstream where Word and Spirit operate as one.

If we are immersed in the eternal life of God, then

nothing else in this life can (ultimately) harm us. So, however great the floods may be, however wild the storm, with the Psalmist we may rejoice that:

> God is our refuge and strength,
>> an ever present help in trouble.
> Therefore we will not fear, though the earth
>> give way,
>> and the mountains fall into the heart of the sea,
> though its waters roar and foam
>> and the mountains quake with their surging.
> There is a river whose streams
>> make glad the city of God,
> the holy place, where the Most High dwells.
>> God is within her, she will not fall:
> God will help her at break of day.
>
> (Psalm 46.1–5)

For further reflection

1. In what ways do you feel influenced by the interface between earth, air and sea? Do you find such places refreshing? If so in what ways? Do you ever sense a battle going on there between opposing forces? Read Psalm 46 again, What does it make you feel? Turn your thoughts about it into a prayer.

2. If you are not as 'good with animals' as Guthlac seems to have been, why do you think this might be?

3. If you were in the crowd listening to John the Baptist, what would you be feeling? Consider what Jesus meant when he said:

'We played the flute for you and you did
not dance; we sang a dirge, and you did not
mourn.' For John came neither eating nor
drinking, and they say, 'He has a demon'.
The Son of Man came eating and drinking, and they say, 'Here is a glutton and a
drunkard, a friend of tax collectors and
"sinners"'. But wisdom is proved right by
her actions.

(Matthew 11.16–19)

4. Which of the following issues is the most
   important nowadays: infant baptism; indiscrimi-
   nate baptism; baptism of the Holy Spirit; understanding the difference between bapting and
   baptizing? What do you feel about your own
   experience of baptism?
5. Why did Jesus present himself for baptism? Why
   was John unwilling to agree to do this? How do
   you think Jesus' baptism was connected with the
   vision of the Spirit coming as a dove, and leading
   Jesus to be tempted in the wilderness (Matthew
   3.13–4.1)?

3
Wisdom in the Wilderness

————•◦◦⊙◦◦•————

THE WILDERNESS FEATURES IN THE BIBLE as an interface where significant events unfold, spiritual insight is
enriched, vision is renewed, wisdom grows, and the true
nature of life's real treasure is disclosed. In the Sinai
desert God held council with Moses and gave Israel
their first taste of freedom, guiding them with his Spirit
and teaching them through the Law. The Judaean
wilderness, scene of Jesus' fasting and temptation, is still
a very wild place. It is as dangerous to get lost there now
as it was when Jesus told the story of the man who fell
among thieves, when religious functionaries ignored
him and hurried by, and a humble Samaritan did his
good deed.

Wonderful wild places still exist in Britain on our own
islands, some bearing witness to spiritual adventurers of
earlier days: Columba's Iona, Aidan's Lindisfarne – and
one which naturalist Mike Tomkies has called the 'last
wild place', Loch Shiel, haunt of wildcat and golden
eagle on whose tiny Eilean Fhionnan strange tomb-
stones seem to lean across, watching you as you row by;
while Saint Finnan's Celtic bell still stands on a stone
altar open to the skies, chained to the wall and protected
from theft by the threat of an ancient curse! From 1687
till his death in 1724, Alexander MacDonald lived there,
at Dalilea House – a man of immense physical strength,

47

and powerful intellect to match. He would row the
narrows to serve his islet church, and tramp the 30 miles
across the bogs and braes of Ardnamurchan, to preach in
Kilchoan, his other parish. In 1729 his son Alasdair
MacMhaighstir Alasdair was appointed Eilean Fhionnan's
teacher and ceister (catechist) by the Society for the
Propagation of Christian Knowledge. He was to become
one of the greatest Gaelic poets, official bard to Prince
Charles Edward, and his first companion when he sailed
up the Loch in 1745, to raise the Standard at Glenfinnan.[1]

The perils of the wilderness

Nearer home, around the Wash stretch marshlands, sanc-
tuaries for wildlife, or test ranges for aerial bombardment.
The wild Wash, its shoals, its Roaring Middle and its
estuaries are a haven for the soul as well as for the seals
and wildfowl. After a spell in the marshes, one returns to
civilization with perceptions sharpened for the demands
of daily life. In the wilderness, we can discover spiritual
treasure. Saint Mark begins his Gospel with the quotation:
'I will send my messenger . . . a voice of one calling in
the desert, "Prepare the way for the Lord . . ."'.

What is it about the wilderness which feeds the soul?
The wilderness has its own rules and rhythms of life. For
example, in the solitude of the marshlands we have to
retune ourselves, using all our senses, because out on the
saltings, we feel nervous. The ground under our feet is
not entirely secure. The creeks, with their overhanging
banks cut by the tides, are deceptive, ready to give way
as we get ready to jump. They are much deeper than we
thought, and are lined with glutinous dark mud and

slippery ooze. To enjoy all its riches, we need to respond appropriately to the nature of the place.

The samphire, purslane, sea lavender and clumps of shrubby sea-blight grow there according to Nature's laws, not ours. Rotten posts of decayed piers, like old bones in the landscape remind us that sea and swamp can in time obliterate all our attempts to tame it.

And yet the wilderness is not wholly alien to us. When we spend time in such a place, thinking it will be foreign to our nature, we are surprised to find that we have a real affinity with what is there, something primal and arcane. True, in winter, as we walk beside the wetlands, our domesticated background makes us feel that this khaki landscape is dismal and forlorn, a feeling Keats evoked in 'La Belle Dame Sans Merci':

> The sedge is withered from the lake,
> And no bird sings.[2]

Yet we can learn to look at this scene in a new way. We can see the withered reeds and sedges with their razor edges are a resource which our ancestors would have appreciated as thatching for their marshy mud and wattle dwellings, keeping them warm and dry. When spring arrives, and the marshes trill, buzz and croak with life again, their dead fronds too will give way to sturdy greenery, with brown and yellow inflorescence.

The inter-tidal arena of the Wash is another mysterious wilderness. One moment, it extends a sunny greeting to the walker, who plods out from the beach to splash over the sand and mud for a mile or two, until the houses look tiny like toys. A few hours later, and the sea has crept back in. From the beach a local canoeist sometimes paddles far out to net fish round the emerging sandbanks. Even for him, the Wash has its dangers. One day the tide crept up as he waded with his drag-net. With water up to his chest, the only way back into the boat was to turn it sideways, letting it fill with water, then climb in and frantically bale it out again. In every wilderness, we need to be alert to the dangers.

The wilderness demands humility. Those who overlook this do so at their peril, as the story of King John reminds us. The Norfolk journalist, Bruce Robinson, grew up in this area. He describes how in the days when the North Sea was called the German Ocean, the Wash estuary reached far south into Cambridgeshire, driving a wedge between 'the sing-song dialects of Norfolk and the harsher tones of Lincolnshire', and was called the Wellstream. To avoid a long detour, travellers had to cross it and, unless they were very foolish, would follow a Wash guide with his long staff. John, harassed by civil strife after Magna Carta, was causing havoc in Lincolnshire. Wealthy Lynn was on his side. He arrived there on 11 October 1216 to ship supplies north, and feasted so well that his health suffered. The next day he ordered his retinue to cross the Wellstream, while he hastened to Wisbech to conclude more business, taking the long way round to meet them. Some 3,000 knights, staff, servants, courtiers, horses, carts and wagons, against expert advice, but fearing his anger should they be delayed, crossed too soon on a falling tide, and were bogged down in the insufficiently drained sands and muddy creeks. As a contemporary writer put it, 'a whirlpool in the middle of the water absorbed all into its depths'. John, suffering from dysentery, died at Newark the next week. His treasures still lie buried, probably under 30 feet of mud. [3]

Wisdom and treasure

In his impatience and failure to understand the nature of the marshland, King John demonstrated his proverbial lack of wisdom – and wisdom is the greatest treasure: 'Wisdom is supreme; therefore get wisdom. Though it cost all you have, get understanding ... she will set a garland of grace on your head and present you with a crown of splendour' (Proverbs 4.7, 9). Many proverbs extol its worth: 'Wisdom is more precious than rubies, nothing you desire can compare with her. Long life is in her right hand; in her left hand are riches and honour. Her ways are pleasant ways, and all her paths are peace' (Proverbs 3.15–17), never forgetting that 'The fear of the Lord is the beginning of wisdom, and knowledge of the Holy One is understanding' (Proverbs 9.10).

Through wisdom, we come to see that God delights to surprise us, and wisdom helps us to understand how this is his way. In Matthew 13.44–46, Jesus taught that the Kingdom of God was like treasure. One person stumbles on it, hidden in a field, while another only finds his perfect pearl after a long search. The important point was that once they have found it, they give it the first place in their life.

The country round the Wash has treasure stories to tell, and some wisdom on how to find it. Snettisham is famous for treasure. The village cosily nestling beneath its hill, with its farms, its school, its shops, inns, church and chapels, its houses and its coastline ... these are a general treasure which all can enjoy. It also has a special treasure, and the village sign gleams with a replica of its golden necklace, or torc, highlight of a hoard now on display in Norwich Castle and in the British Museum. In 1948 a field of lavender on the Ken Hill estate was being turned over to barley, with the new deep-ploughing technique. A young tractor driver struck treasure. He did not recognize it. The mud-encrusted objects looked like parts of an old brass bedstead, and were left to lie at the roadside for a fortnight. In 1950 another tractor brought up the most famous haul, of which the Snettisham great torc is one of Britain's greatest Celtic antiquities. It is a solid 'necklace', 3 lb 7 oz of electrum (three parts gold, two of silver), and is made of eight thick strands, each composed of eight wires tightly intertwined. This 'torc' is then welded into 'terminals', to which beautifully chased and engraved ornaments were added after they had been cast, forming a characteristic trademark of the 'Snettisham' style. Examples have been found as far away as Somerset, Staffordshire and Peebles. A tiny Celtic gold coin hidden in the torc dates it to about 70 BC. The field has become known as the Gold (or Treasure) Field, for until 1992 finds continued to be made, up to a total of 180 torcs, not all complete, together with many other fragments which suggest that this was the 'factory' of a brilliant artist of the Iceni. A hundred years later, their queen, Boadicea, wore a great twisted neck-ring or large gold necklace, according to the Roman historian Dio Cassius. These treasures were buried in carrstone 'pits', a foot below the rust-coloured soil. A Roman household built nearby soon after these times was oblivious to what lay so near at hand. Bruce Robinson refers to a folk tale that golden gates were buried in a field near Heacham, the centre of the lavender industry; while Flitcham (Felix's 'ham'), near Sandringham, had a field once called Drakenhowe, or Dragon's Hill – and, of course, dragons always live near gold!

Such discoveries remind us how often we continue to scratch out our meagre life while undreamed-of spiritual riches lie beneath our feet. Swaffham, along the road from Lynn to Norwich, reminds us that we may need to look at life from a different angle before we can recognize the hidden treasures which lie so close to hand. Swaffham's sign is not a golden anything, but John Chapman, the Pedlar of Swaffham, who travelled far to find a treasure in his own backyard. He had a dream which convinced him to go to London to find his fortune. Leaving his 'pad' (pedlar's wicker basket) behind, but with his dog on a lead, and a stout staff in his hand, he tramped the hundred miles to London Bridge. There he hung around, arousing the suspicion of a local shopkeeper. When he sheepishly told the shopkeeper his dream, the man laughed him to scorn 'Why!' he cried, 'If I dreamed such a dream, I would pay it no heed, even if it had gold under a flagstone by an apple tree in my own back yard!' John made his way home, discouraged. But it struck him as odd that the man had mentioned a flagstone by an apple tree as his backyard had an apple tree and a few old flagstones in it. He dug by the tree, and what should he find but an old pot, with grimy lettering on the lid, and gold coins inside. He took the coins, and studied the lettering which looked like Latin, but he did not know what they meant. So he copied the words out on a piece of paper, put it in his window, and sat down to listen. After a while, he heard someone read the words, and then

add: 'Under me is more'. John duly dug – and found
an even bigger hoard. He became Churchwarden, and
built the splendid North Aisle of the church, with seven
bays and thirteen Tudor-arch windows, and carved on
two pew-ends you can see the Pedlar and his dog.[4]

Where the treasure of wisdom is concerned, it is not
the setting which is important, but whether we are open
to the activity of the Holy Spirit, as Paul reminds us:

> We speak of God's secret wisdom, a wisdom that has
> been hidden and that God destined for our glory
> before time began. None of the rulers of this age
> understood it, for if they had, they would not have
> crucified the Lord of glory. However as it is written:
> 'No eye has seen, no ear has heard, no mind has
> conceived what God has prepared for those who love
> him.' But God has revealed it to us by his Spirit.
>
> (1 Corinthians 2.7–10)

Jesus' temptations in the wilderness

All the same, the wilderness was an important setting
where God revealed treasures of his wisdom to his people.
Paul spent time in Arabia after his Damascus experience
(Galatians 1.17). Jesus fasted and was tempted there.
John the Baptist lived there; and long before all that, it
was in the wilderness that the twelve tribes of Israel
were forged into a nation. Until then, they had been an
enslaved and dispirited minority, slaves in the high culture
of Egypt. After forty years, they were ready to enjoy the
land of Canaan, and in the process they had experienced
in embryo each of the three issues which Jesus himself
faced, when, after he had been baptized, 'the Spirit sent

him out into the desert, and he was in the desert for
forty days, being tempted by Satan. He was with the
wild animals, and angels attended him' (Mark 1.12–13).

There, in the desert, he prayed and contemplated the
full meaning of what he had accepted in baptism, and at
the end of the 40-day period, this process culminated in
his temptation by the Devil. Satan (Hebrew: 'accuser')
tempts us, in order to destroy God's work. God allows
this to happen, to strengthen our faith and deepen our
understanding: 'After fasting for forty days and forty
nights, he was hungry. The tempter came to him and
said, "If you are the Son of God, tell these stones to
become bread"' (Matthew 4.2–3).

Long ago, the Israelites had once been hungry too:

In the desert the whole community grumbled
against Moses and Aaron . . . 'If only we had died by
the Lord's hand in Egypt! There we sat round pots of
meat and ate all the food we wanted, but you have
brought us out into this desert to starve this entire
assembly to death.' Then the Lord said to Moses, 'I
will rain down bread from heaven for you.' . . . In the
morning there was a layer of dew around the camp.
When the dew was gone, thin flakes like frost on the
ground appeared on the desert floor. When the
Israelites saw it, they said to each other, 'What is it?'
For they did not know. . . The people of Israel called
the bread manna.

(Exodus 16.1–4, 13–15, 31)

'Manna' means 'What is it?' Later Moses explained the
lesson God had taught them:

Remember how the Lord your God led you all the
way in the desert these forty years, to humble you

and to test you in order to know what was in your
heart . . . He humbled you, causing you to hunger
and then feeding you with manna . . . in order to
teach you that man does not live on bread alone but
on every word that comes from the mouth of the
Lord.

(Deuteronomy 8.2–3)

'Man shall not live on bread alone.' It was with this text
that Jesus armed himself as he fought off the first temptation. His priority was to do the will of God. Saint John
.ecords Jesus' total commitment to his Father's purposes,
and the progressive way in which God rewarded his
faithfulness:

> I tell you the truth, the Son can do nothing by him-
> self; he can do only what he sees his Father doing,
> because whatever the Father does the Son also does.
> For the Father loves the Son and shows him all he
> does. Yes, to your amazement he will show him even
> greater things than these. For just as the Father raises
> the dead and gives them life, even so the Son gives
> life to whom he is pleased to give it . . . I seek not to
> please myself but him who sent me.
>
> (John 5.19–21, 30)

Jesus was hungry, but by faith he received support
through the power of God. On another occasion, he
startled his disciples with the words: 'My food is to do
the will of him who sent me and to finish his work'
(John 4.34).

The Russian novelist Dostoevsky commented on the
story of Jesus' temptation in The Legend of the Grand
Inquisitor,[5] which he saw as the culminating point of his

literary life. It is a story told by Ivan to his brother Aloyisha, in the book *The Brothers Karamazov*. The Grand Inquisitor, aged and wizened, but still with riveting eyes, has just burned 100 heretics in front of the populace of sixteenth-century Seville, when he is brought face to face with 'him' – an almost silent visitor to the city, whose gentle eyes shine with compassion, and who raises a girl, dead in her mother's arms, to life. The stranger is arrested, and in the dark of a night heavy with the scent of lemon and laurel, the Inquisitor enters his cell, and begins a breath-taking indictment against 'him' and his offer of freedom to humanity. The monologue that follows has been described by critics in a variety of ways, ranging from a repudiation of God, a presentation of the human predicament, a discussion of power and totalitarianism, and an image of the arrogance of organized religion.

The story of Jesus' temptation, says the Grand Inquisitor, is itself a miracle. If the disciples had not learned it, if it had been lost, not all the most brilliant sages of the world could have thought up so profound yet simple a key to human history, and to all that would transpire down the ages that would follow. Satan had put his finger unerringly on the three greatest truths about the human situation: our demand for bread, mystery, and authority.

For Jesus to offer people freedom rather than bread was madness. While people love to imagine they are free, they reject the burden of uncertainty which real freedom brings – unless they are well off. First give them food, and only then ask them to be virtuous. To live only for a 'bread from heaven', to be free in a way which scorns the pangs of hunger, is too much to ask. Once they are threatened with starvation, people will

come running to lay down their liberty at the feet of
any dictator who promises to feed them.

Fyodor Dostoevsky (1821–81) was writing at a time
when revolution of one sort or another was in the air.
Liberalism was at its height, but Marxism was coming
into being. Jesus, however, embodied a different approach.
He offered no philosophy, as such. Instead, he offered
himself together with his teaching: 'If you hold to my
teaching, you are really my disciples. Then you will
know the truth, and the truth will set you free' (John
8.31). The truth he taught demanded faith, and again it
centred on himself. For all those who were willing to
'come to him', he promised God's gift of inner power
and peace. Jesus' claims created storms of protest from
religious leaders. They demanded proof: 'What will you
do?' they asked, 'Our forefathers ate the manna in the
desert; as it is written "He gave them bread from heaven
to eat"' (John 6.30–31). 'Jesus replied, "I am the bread
of life. He who comes to me will never go hungry, and
he who believes in me will never be thirsty"'(John
6.35).

God's revelation promises the renewal of human
nature from within. It is not a law of the old sort, carved
in stone, and outwardly enforced. Jesus, therefore, did
not only teach about the 'bread of life', he had to be the
bread himself, and that in turn meant being 'broken
bread': 'This bread is my flesh which I will give for the
life of the world' (John 6.51). Later, he put the same
truth even more directly:

> The hour has come for the Son of Man to be glori-
> fied. I tell you the truth, unless an ear of wheat falls
> to the ground and dies, it remains only a single seed.
> But if it dies, it produces many seeds. The man who

loves his life will lose it, while the man who hates his
life in this world will keep it for eternal life.

(John 12.23–25)

Suppose a visitor from outer space wished to know
what food we live on, we would say 'bread is the "staff
of life"' and show them a grain of wheat. They might
ask how it is made – by polymerizing amino-acids,
perhaps? 'No!' we would reply, 'We take it out and drop
it on the muddy ground.' Could anyone believe it? Is it
not ridiculous? But . . . that really is the way to do it.
'Unless an ear of wheat falls into the ground and dies, it
will not bear fruit' – and we would soon go hungry
otherwise! Jesus, the Bread from Heaven, had only one
way to go if he was to be our Bread of Life.

At this point, I believe we can learn something
important from the idea of bread as 'manna'. We may
say, now, in the light of Jesus, that manna represents a
giant question mark. 'Manna', as we saw, means 'what is
it?' And it is only when we wake up and start to ask the
right questions, that we begin to find what it really
means to have God at the centre of everything. If Jesus
is to be 'our bread from heaven', our 'manna', we must
learn to put a question mark over every aspect of life,
and apply the light that comes from Christ to everything.
This does not mean we are to go through life perpetu-
ally worried and indecisive. But, in seeking God's will,
we should approach life with 'confident uncertainty', if
we are to discover, often the hard way, what God's will
really is. For we may be sure that though the learning
curve is onerous, God has guaranteed that faithfulness
will be rewarded – with greater freedom and further
understanding!

The wilderness experience reminds us that we learn

these lessons best when we have to make do without
relying on the 'conveniences' of the world we live in. We
do not own our possessions, but far more often they own
us, emprison our lives, and supplant the real treasure
God has in store for us. So, like the distinguished physicist Ernest Rutherford (1871–1937), we should rather
be glad to say: 'We have no money, so we shall have to
think!'

There was an intriguing obituary in *The Independent*
of one man who memorably illustrates this principle:

Capt Nigel Willmott RN, born Simla, 12.7.1910,
died Paphos 26.6.1992

When in 1940 the enemy became master of the
entire coastline of Europe, the Royal Navy as a whole
did not give much thought about how they were
going to get the army back into Europe; they believed
they had a lot of other more pressing problems.

But one junior naval officer, Lt. Cdr. Nigel
Willmott, a navigator, had a motto: *People would rather
die than think. Many of them do.* He thought about
the problems, realized that is was going to be much
more difficult than had been generally appreciated,
would need very special skills and training, and was
of enormous importance. Naval officers are trained
to avoid beaches. Now beaches would have to be
located – obviously, at night – reconnoitred – obviously, by both sailors and soldiers, again at night
– and found again on the night of the assault. What
preparations were being made to accomplish this?
None at all. And for some time no one listened to
Willmott.

He knew that for a start it would mean swimming,

probably from a submarine. So he began swimming
25 lengths every morning in the Cairo Club Baths –
he was stationed in Cairo. There he found a Com-
mando officer called Courtney, who before the war
had hunted African big game from a foldboat. A
foldboat could pass through a submarine's hatch . . .
Willmott kept telling senior officers that charts were
often wrong – they were intended to keep people
away from the shore – and sand moved, and a recon-
naissance from the periscope of a submarine a mile
offshore was not enough. Still no one listened.

In 1942, Operation Torch took place – the North
African landings. No one landed on the right beach
and many landed eight or more miles out of position.
If the invasion had been opposed, it would have been
a catastrophe. It was just what Willmott had been
predicting. He was sent for by Mountbatten, now
Chief of Combined Operations, and told to set up
the organization he required with top priority. It
was called COPP – 'Combined Operations Pilotage
Parties', a name chosen to hide its real functions.

When detailed planning for the invasion of Europe
was taking place, an admiral at one meeting asked
whether the sand on a beach under discussion was
suitable for tanks. The Intelligence Officer said:

'Actually, sir, one of our officers was there last
night. Willmott, will you come in?' And in he came,
very short of sleep, with a core of the beach sand
which had already been analysed and showed that it
was suitable. COPP parties took lines of soundings,
measured gradients, investigated defences, checked
beach exits and finally marked the landing-places on
the night (in the case of Normandy, sitting in midget
submarines) for every major landing from Sicily

onwards, including crossing the Rhine and in Burma. How many soldiers' lives were saved by Willmott's prescience and persistence cannot be calculated .[6]

The story of Nigel Wilmott's hard-headed determination clearly shows us that the burden of freedom demands our total commitment, and reinforces the warnings Jesus gave his followers: 'The people of this world are more shrewd in dealing with their own kind than are the people of the light' (Luke 16.8). 'I am sending you out like sheep among wolves. Therefore be as shrewd as snakes and as innocent as doves' (Matthew 10.16).

The second temptation

How can we maintain the sustained effort which such costly faith in God seems to demand? The Inquisitor was convinced it was impossible, at least for the vast majority of humanity. However, the second temptation shows there is a way. Once again, it parallels Israel's experience in the wilderness, in the way in which God cared for them:

> By day the Lord went ahead of them in a pillar of cloud to guide them on their way and by night in a pillar of fire to give them light . . . Neither the pillar of cloud by day nor the pillar of fire by night left its place in front of the people . . . Then the angel of God, who had been travelling in front, withdrew and went behind them. The pillar of cloud also moved from in front and stood behind them, coming between the armies of Egypt and Israel.
>
> (Exodus 13.21–22, 14.19–20)

Later in the Bible, Isaiah develops the meaning of this divine activity:

> I will tell of the kindnesses of the Lord . . . yes, the many good things he has done for the house of Israel . . . He said, 'Surely they are my people, sons who will not be false to me'; and so he became their Saviour. In all their distress he too was distressed, and the angel of his presence saved them. In his love and mercy he redeemed them: he lifted them up and carried them all the days of old. Yet they rebelled and grieved his Holy Spirit.
>
> (Isaiah 63.7–10)

We must bear these Old Testament references in mind, as we turn to the second temptation, where Satan took Jesus to the highest point of the Temple, and said: 'If you are the Son of God . . . throw yourself down. For it is written: "He will command his angels concerning you, and they will lift you up in their hands so that you will not strike your foot against a stone"' (Matthew 4.6, quoting Psalm 91.11–12). However, Jesus knew that what was important was not some sensational demonstration of his divine status, defying the laws of gravity, but that he should truly be God's Son, obeying him. The Devil deceitfully omitted the fundamental conditions which surround this promise. They emphasize the need to 'live in' God and love Him: 'If you make the Most High your dwelling . . . then no harm will befall you . . . "Because he loves me," says the Lord, "I will rescue him . . ."' (Psalm 91.9, 14).

In making God his dwelling place, and in living in God's love, Jesus believed that he had come to set people free, not from the laws of physics, but from what

Saint Paul calls the 'law of sin and death', something Paul had known all too much about in his own earlier frustrated life:

> So I find this law at work: when I want to do good, evil is right there with me. For in my inner being I delight in God's law; but I see another law at work in the members of my body, waging war against the law of my mind and making me a prisoner of the law of sin at work within my members. What a wretched man I am! Who will rescue me from this body of death? . . . Thanks be to God through Jesus Christ our Lord! . . . through Christ Jesus the law of the Spirit of life set me free from the law of sin and death.
>
> (Romans 7.21–25, 8.2)

If Jesus was to free us, by opening the way for the Spirit of life to carry us, as the Angel Spirit had done in those far off days for Israel, then Jesus on his part had to surrender his life and liberty, and this he willingly agreed to do. What he affirmed in the wilderness, he accepted in Gethsemane, and adhered to on the cross, where we read that:

> Those who passed by hurled insults at him, shaking their heads and saying, 'So! You who are going to destroy the temple and build it in three days, come down from the cross and save yourself!' In the same way the chief priests and the teachers of the law mocked him among themselves. 'He saved others,' they said, 'but he can't save himself! Let this Christ, this King of Israel, come down now from the cross, that we may see and believe.' Those crucified with him also heaped insults on him. (Mark 15.29–32)

As Katherine Kelly's hymn puts it:

> Was it the nails, O Saviour,
> That bound Thee to the tree?
> Nay, 'twas Thine everlasting love
> Thy love for me, for me.[7]

In all of this, Jesus rejected two powerful inducements: first, he refused to free himself from the way that would lead to his crucifixion; and second, he refused to perform a spectacular miracle, leaping from the Temple, in order to create belief among the crowds, and give the leaders the proof they kept demanding. The freedom he embodied and taught was a freedom from all material and spiritual constraints, other than those freely chosen in response to the love and holiness of God.

The Grand Inquisitor declares that there is one situation where people will give up their lust for bread. It is when they find someone who can gain control over their consciences.

> The mystery of human life is not only in living but in knowing why one lives. Without a clear idea of what he is to live for, man will not consent to live and will rather destroy himself than remain on the earth, though he were surrounded by loaves of bread. And what became of it? Instead of gaining possession of their freedom, you gave them greater freedom than ever!
>
> There are three forces, the only three forces that are able to conquer and hold captive for ever the conscience of these weak rebels for their own happiness. These forces are: miracle, mystery, and authority – you rejected all three, and yourself set the example for doing so.

Miracle compels belief, and Jesus refused to build his kingdom on those lines. As the Grand Inquisitor continues:

> You did not come down from the cross, because again
> you did not want to enslave man by a miracle, and
> because you hungered for a faith based on free-will,
> not miracles. You hungered for a freely given love,
> and not for the servile raptures of the slave before the
> might that has terrified him once and for all – but
> again your judgement of men was too high, for they
> are slaves, though rebels by nature.

Although Jesus did often demonstrate the power of the
coming of the Kingdom of God through miracles, he
pointedly and persistently refused to do so in regard to
his own existence, or in the costly process of redemption,
or in answering the demand to prove himself. The
Inquisitor is right in saying that Jesus rejected the use of
miracle, mystery and authority and all the hypocrisy it
carries in its wake.

Where the Inquisitor tragically misses the point,
however, is in failing to understand that true faith is not
about screwing up the will, following the distant example
of Jesus, as if to be some latter-day heroic Stoic. Instead,
it is all about having child-like faith to receive the grace
of God, which through the Holy Spirit was also the
secret of Jesus' triumphant power. This same grace and
Holy Presence are available to all who will step out in
faith, and trust themselves to God.

To the onlooker, viewing faith from the outside it
must be hard to distinguish between moral strenuousness
and committed faith, or to know that the former, based
on self-effort, leads to despair or hypocrisy, while the
other, even when seemingly defeated, will always rise

again, growing under adversity. To such a person, one can only say with the David of old: 'Taste and see that the Lord is good; blessed is the man who takes refuge in him . . . for those who fear him lack nothing' (Psalm 34.8–9). The second temptation shows us, then, that there is inner strength available, a baptism of the Holy Spirit. Without this inward power, and in our own strength, we are indeed bound to fail, and fall into despair, as Dostoevsky indicated.

The third temptation

How, though, was Jesus to convince the world that God's gift of inner power does indeed exist? The third temptation focuses on the answer to this question, and corresponds to the Old Testament moment when Moses finally stood on the Pisgah of Mount Nebo, and God told him to view the promised land (Deuteronomy 34.1–4). What a view it was, reaching in the north to the towering peak of Mount Hermon, covered with perpetual snow, and from there stretching south, across the panorama of Galilee and the Golan, along the great ridge of central Israel, Mount Ebal and Mount Gerizim, passing on south over what would become David's city of Jerusalem, and on again over Bethel and Bethlehem, then rising to the heights of Hebron, before falling, falling to the Negeb, the desert of the Arabah and distant Sinai. Far below his feet lay the winding valley of the Jordan, part of the Great Rift Valley, leading to the Dead Sea, shimmering in a haze of heat.

In the third temptation, however, Satan put to Jesus a far, far greater vision, as from so high a peak that he could 'show him all the kingdoms of the world and their splendour'. 'All this will I give you,' he said, 'if you will bow down and worship me' (Matthew 4.9). How Jesus' heart must have gone out to those far-flung empires, nations, peoples. And yet Jesus could also see that all that splendour was but skin-deep. It was a glory built by tyrants on the backs of slaves. It was a splendour that was based on arrogance, greed, malice and revenge. He knew that Satan's ways could never deliver Satan's kingdom into the glorious liberty of the Sons of Light. To do that, an entirely new sort of kingdom must be born, based on love, mutual respect and solid truth. It must be a kingdom where God was the builder, and the centre of everything.

The Grand Inquisitor believed Jesus should have taken the sword of Caesar from the Devil's hand, and used his power to weld the kingdoms of the world in one great empire, ruled with an iron fist. But God's plan is that his Kingdom shall be built on freedom, love and justice, growing out of the loyalty of those whose freedom continues to grow. The only way to inspire such loyalty, and build it so true that even the gates of hell could not prevail against it, was to build it through the cross, creating a bond of undying love that nothing could destroy. John 12 has Jesus' final answer to Satan's most powerful temptation: '..."Now is the time for judgement on this world; now the prince of this world will be driven out. But I, when I am lifted up from the earth, will draw all men to myself." He said this to show what kind of death he was going to die' (John 12.31–33). John's use of language is always subtle, often ironic. 'When I am lifted up' is a case in point: it is a phrase that could be used for a coronation, for someone lifted up onto a throne; but it is also a word for crucifixion, for someone being hoisted aloft for a brutal execution. Jesus' crown of thorns symbolizes the amazing paradox.

We can see this love at work on someone who began by vigorously repudiating it: St Paul, whose eventual recognition of what Jesus had done for him was radically transforming:

> Christ's love compels us, because we are convinced that one died for all, and therefore all died. And he died for all, that those who live should no longer live for themselves but for him who died for them and was raised again . . . if anyone is in Christ, he is a new creation: the old has gone, the new has come . . . God was reconciling himself to us . . . and he has committed to us the message of reconciliation.
>
> (2 Corinthians 5.14–18)

We have moved a long way from the wilderness, but we have arrived at an entirely new creation. We have seen how pitting our wits against the unsettling strangeness of the wilderness sharpens our perceptions. Our inability to tame it teaches us humility. Our frailty in the face of it moves us to seek after wisdom, and wisdom opens the door to God's treasures, which are otherwise locked away, unrecognized, unreachable, hidden 'in our own backyard'. We saw how Jesus' temptations resonated with earlier truths, and that bringing them together helps us understand Jesus' death and resurrection. The next chapter moves on to see how Jesus brings us 'home' to God, in what so often can seem to be an alien and hostile universe.

For further reflection

1. What do you value most in life? Has it always been the same? How do you think your feeling about this might change in the future?

2. Do you think the story of the Pedlar of Swaffham is mythical? What treasure do you feel might be hidden, so far unrecognized, 'in your backyard'? Has 'going away', in any sense, ever helped to make you more aware of the true value of something you had previously taken for granted?

3. In the light of what was said about Jesus as the bread of life, what do you learn from the connection between: (a) 'manna'; (b) Jesus' temptation to turn stones into bread; and (c) Jesus' parable of the seed that only produces a harvest when it dies? Can you develop a prayer out of what you feel about this? What difference do you think may come about if you pray that prayer?

4. What do you think Paul meant when he said (a) 'When I want to do good, evil is right there with me'; and (b) 'through Christ Jesus the law of the Spirit of life set me free from the law of sin and death' (Romans 7.21, 8.2)?

5. In this chapter, Moses' view of the promised land (from Mount Nebo, before he died, Deuteronomy 34.1–4), was linked to Jesus' view of the world when the devil offered to give him all its kingdoms (Matthew 4.8–10), and Jesus' belief that when he was lifted up on the cross he would draw all people to himself (John 12.32–33). What can we learn from linking themes in the Bible story together in this way?

4

Homing in

~~~~~~ ◦◉◦ ~~~~~~

God is our eternal home

IN THE PREVIOUS CHAPTER we explored how Jesus'
wilderness experience prepared him to fulfil God's
work, bringing us the bread of life, opening the way for
the coming of the Holy Spirit, and establishing the
Kingdom of God. How, then, can it all become real for
us in our day? The answer is summed up in a modern
prayer, which says: 'when we were far off you met us in
your Son and brought us home' (Church of England
Alternative Service Book)[1], for it is the Gospel's 'homeliness'
which brings it to life.

We all think we know what 'home' is, and talk of
'home, sweet home' and tell each other that 'an English-
man's home is his castle'. Some dwellings are only stag-
ing posts, though not all homes have to be fixed – for
centuries gypsies have had their homes on the move.
Queen Alexandra surely wanted her bungalow to be a
homely place – in Denmark, as elsewhere, 'homeliness'
is a most important factor in their culture, and conjures
up visions of welcome, security, nurture, and close personal relationships.

The connotation of the word 'home' takes on an even
greater depth when we focus on its spiritual dimension.
Neither Greek nor Hebrew has a word for 'home' in the
way we have, but the Bible lifts the essential idea to the

highest level, using various related words. One word it uses is 'refuge' or 'dwelling place', as in Moses' final blessing on the tribes of Israel, 'The eternal God is your refuge, and underneath are the everlasting arms' (Deuteronomy 33.27). Psalm 90, also ascribed to Moses, begins: 'Lord, you have been our dwelling place thoughout all generations' (Psalm 90.1).

This psalm goes on to contrast God's eternal being, with the brevity of human life, 'Before the mountains were born, or you brought forth the earth and the world, from everlasting to everlasting you are God. You turn men back to dust, saying "Return to dust, O sons of men." For a thousand years in your sight are like a day that has just gone by, or like a watch in the night' (Psalm 90.2–4).

Our human transience and God's eternal transcendence are complementary aspects of this homely picture, and it is a universal human instinct. When Paul was talking to the Athenians, he was happy to borrow this idea from their own writers, 'From one man God made every nation . . . so that men would seek him and perhaps reach out for him and find him, though he is not far from each one of us. "For in him we live and move and have our being." As some of your own poets have said, "We are his offspring"' (Acts 17.26–28).

Of course, in the natural world, the homing instinct is basic. Just as the great starscapes which hang over the Wash on a clear frosty night move like clockwork round Polaris, the Pole Star, so the wildfowl, the waders and the passerines come and go according to their season. There is something reassuring about their regularity. As Jeremiah noted, they 'know' and they 'obey': 'Even the stork in the sky knows her appointed seasons, and the dove, the swift and the thrush observe the time of their migration' (Jeremiah 8.7). Thousands of birds make the Wash their home, travelling thousands of miles to home in on their favourite habitat, coming north for summer nesting, or retreating from the Arctic night. Some just flop down for a rest, a drink and a bite to eat, before setting off again. It is astonishing to watch the great autumnal stream of fieldfares and redwings, like clouds of gorgeous locusts, flowing all day long across the Country Park, over the ponds, skimming our roof, the Scalp and the Wash – some going west, others peeling off and wheeling south.

As many as 20,000 knot come south to spend the winter, and at very high tides end up packed into one dense grey mass on the Strand, a curving shingle bank on the reserve. There are three hides, where keen bird-watchers can remain and observe this natural wonder. As the tide ebbs, and the marshes reappear, the birds rise as one and surge forth in a great whirring cloud to swoop only a few feet above your head if you are in the right place. And yet, once the summer comes, they will almost all have gone. The dunlin also make the beach their winter home, starting to arrive in August, still wearing their chestnut waistcoats, back from the incomparable daylight of the Arctic summer, which so richly teems with fauna and flora on the edge of the ice-bound ocean, where narwhal, gyrfalcon, musk ox and polar bear live their mysterious lives. The dunlin settle down at once to probe the mud, and roost on the Scalp, as if travelling a few thousand miles were nothing at all.

While the winter birds use the Wash as a magnificent refuge, it is the summer birds whose instincts make the place a real home. They build their nests or scratch out their scrapes, lay their eggs, and raise their young there. Swallow, ring plover, nightjar (even golden oriole, though not so near at hand), come north for our spring and summer sunshine. I hope the nightjars will continue to feel at home on their heath and in the pines. They are fully camouflaged, and can lie all day in the litter, totally invisible. It is a unique experience to stand at nightfall at the foot of their hill, and wait for their strange flight to start. First comes the churring, like a distant mowing machine; then what looks like some giant moth flaps its way above the tree-line, perhaps down to a few feet to have a look at us. They clap their wings, and perch on a branch or wire. Though their numbers have declined, I hope they will continue to sense that this place still has the friendly feel which means welcome and renewal.

Ring plovers lay their eggs in a mere dip on the beach, but the eggs blend so closely with the shingle they are safe, while the parents flutter about nearby giving their lilting 'turwilk' alarm, to distract attention, so that dogs, children and hungry gulls all remain oblivious to what lies only a few feet away. Sadly, they are not always good judges of the tides, and their little homes can get washed away. Skylarks love the Scalp, and lay their eggs in small hollows in a pile of dry seaweed, or under a bush. One flew up from some rubble, and on inspection there were four tiny speckled eggs in a gap under a wedge of concrete. Next week four yellow mouths gaped in the aperture. In no time, they had fledged and flown. A swallow nests in the old hide in the Snettisham Country Park, where the door has fallen off; so while visitors train binoculars on the waders, the swallow flies in and out three feet behind them. She will dart round outside the hide, catch an insect in the wind with a flash of blue and chestnut, swish back in, disappear up into a dark corner of the hide, and in no time will swoop out and be away once more. Sometimes baby seals end up beached, abandoned by their parents who have to leave them if they linger as the tide retreats. Home for them is out on the Seal Sands near Roaring Middle. When you approach, they gaze at you with sorrowful eyes, and even try to flop along behind you when you walk away. The next tide may come too late. But help is available – the Hunstanton Sea Life centre can send someone down to rescue them.

These birds and animals all know their times and seasons, and they obey their instincts faithfully. Our human existence, too, has its rhythms and cycles, and a child's homing instinct is as strong as theirs, as Mother Teresa once observed: 'The home is where the mother is'. On one occasion, when she found what she thought was a destitute child, she

> took him to our children's home, gave him a bath, clean clothes, everything, but after a day the child ran away. Then I said to the sisters, 'Please follow that child.' There under a tree was the mother. She had put two stones under an earthenware vessel and was cooking something she had picked up from the dustbins. The sister asked the child, 'Why did you run away from the home?' And the child said: 'But this is my home, because this is where my mother is.'[2]

Alienation and faith

However, our instincts have a revolutionary additional dimension, the potential (for good or ill) of free will and responsibility. God calls us to come to him for the help we need to fulfil our true potential. But something has gone wrong. We do not want the sort of empowerment God has for us. Contrariness is the symptom of our disenchantment, so that anxiety replaces our confidence and we are alienated instead of feeling at home with God. Jeremiah's up-beat observation of migrating birds ends on a down-beat note, as he grieves for his fellow human beings: 'Even the stork in the sky knows her appointed seasons ... but ... my people do not know the requirements of the Lord' (Jeremiah 8.7). Isaiah shared the same concern, seeing God as a loving father: 'I reared children and brought them up, but they have rebelled against me. The ox knows his master, the donkey his owner's manger, but ... my people do not understand' (Isaiah 1.2–3).

Wordsworth's poem 'Intimations of Immortality', however theologically unorthodox, evokes the sense of nostalgia many Victorians felt as childhood faith gave way to adult scepticism:

> ... trailing clouds of glory do we come
> From God, who is our home:
> Heaven lies about us in our infancy!
> Shades of the prison-house begin to close
> Upon the growing Boy,
> But he beholds the light, and whence it flows,
> He sees it in his joy
> ... at length the Man perceives it die away,
> And fade into the light of common day.[3]

This sense of alienation had not been helped by the rapid growth of knowledge even before Wordsworth's

day. The French mathematician, Blaise Pascal (1623–
1662), was a man of deep religious faith. He, too, was
very much exercised by what the new sciences disclosed
about the universe, 'The eternal silence of those infinite
spaces terrifies me,'[4] and he set out to compose a sys-
tematic answer to the growing attitude of scepticism.
He died having only got as far as a preparatory outline,
his *Pensées*, where he worked out one way to come to
terms with the new situation: by seeing that man, though
physically no longer pivotal to everything, could still be
supreme in respect of his intelligence: 'By space the
Universe encompasses me and swallows me up like a
mere speck; by thought I comprehend the Universe.'[5]

Three centuries have passed since then. Our view of
the cosmos has become far more sophisticated, and the
sense that it is 'there for us' in any personal way, with
God at the centre of it all, has been a matter of continuous debate, with many notable scientists avowing a
strong religious faith in every generation right up to
the present. A prime factor in this debate focuses on
the 'fine-tuning', as it is called, of the cosmos. To put this
in the simplest terms, for example as Professor Russell
Stannard has done so well for children, the initial 'big
bang' was not too little (everything would have collapsed
again by now), and not too much (nothing would have
solidified), but absolutely just right, so that development
could occur at a perfectly balanced rate. The sun is not
too hot, not too cool. To quote him on the remarkable
way in which it appears that a star creates some of the
elements now found on earth, he says:

> Not all the kinds of atom we find on Earth are
> present in the star before the explosion takes place, so

> where do they come from? The answer is that they
> are made during the explosion itself! That's right, it's
> as though the star thinks to itself, 'Whoops! I forgot
> to make some so-and-so; they'll be needing that.' And
> does it at the last minute as everything is on its way
> out.'[6]

However, having faith that God is in control does not
release us from the responsibility he has given us to act
as stewards of the natural order. We would do well to
consider just how vulnerable we become when we act
as if we can do what we like, and refuse to recognize
God, the creator of everything, at the centre of life. Our
little blue-green planetary nest is a precarious place, and
the battle is on to rescue it from the dangers of envi-
ronmental pollution. There is, however, another danger,
that of fatalism, for there is a growing fear that some
astronomical catastrophe could engulf our world, giving
a twenty-first-century twist to the old proverb, 'Let us
eat and drink, for tomorrow we die!' (Isaiah 22.13, and
1 Corinthians 15.32). But once again, faith in God
changes our perspective, so we can calmly, if humbly,
face even such potential cataclysms, if we are convinced
that God really is in control, and has a great and loving
purpose which is unfolding year by year.

Professor Conway-Morris in the 1996 Royal Institu-
tion Christmas Lectures told two such stories. First, there
was the Tunguska Event, in 1908, when the night sky
was lit up by a spectacular display described in a letter to
The Times, from Godmanchester (on the River Ouse).

> Thursday July 2nd: Sir, I should be interested in hear-
> ing whether others of your readers observed the
> strange light in the sky which was seen here last night

by my sister and myself. It was in the North East, and
was of a bright flame colour like the sunrise or sunset.
The sky for some distance above the light, which
appeared to be on the horizon, was blue as in daytime,
with bands of light cloud of a pinkish colour floating
across it at intervals. An hour later, at about 1.30 in
the morning, the room was quite light as if it had
been day.[7]

Four hours later, shock waves were recorded in Cambridge. Something awesome had happened in Siberia.
An elderly man, named Seminov, described what happened overhead:

The sky was split in two, and high above the forest
the whole Northern part of the sky appeared to be
covered in fire. I wanted to pull off my shirt and
throw it away but at that moment there was a bang
in the sky and a mighty crash was heard. I was thrown
to the ground, for a moment I lost consciousness.

For many years, this event remained a mystery. More
recently, its cause has become clear. A meteor, the size of
the Albert Hall, exploded in the atmosphere into tiny
fragments, remnants of which have been discovered in
the rings of a few surviving trees. Had the Tunguska
meteor come four hours later, it would have exploded
over the North Sea, and the shock waves would have
had disastrous consequences all along the British coastline.
However, that would have been insignificant compared
to a catastrophe that took place in prehistoric times.

Professor Conway-Morris's second story told how, in
the 1970s, Louis and Walter Alvarez, father and son, led
the way in revealing the site of an immense meteor collision, traced to Mexico's Yucatan peninsula. Millions of

years ago a huge meteor had struck the earth here, and
sensitive gravitational tests showed the presence of a crater
150 kilometres or more in diameter, a colossal bowl now
filled with lighter sediments, and invisible to the eye.
The effect of the meteor was to release the energy of a
nuclear bomb for every square kilometre of the earth's
surface, concentrated on the impact site. A huge fireball
erupted, vapourizing billions of tons of sulphurous rocks
in the area; the world was enveloped in acid clouds and
blanketed with dust. Thus, 70 per cent of life forms,
including the dinosaurs, were destroyed. It took a million years for the planet to make a full recovery.

In 1977, Monica Grady of the Natural History
Museum suggested that our planet is due a truly massive
collision from either a large asteroid or a long-period
comet. Every year our atmosphere is bombarded by
about 40 tons of small pieces of debris. About a thousand of these rocks are as big as a football; however, most
burn up in their descent, and are seen by us as 'shooting
stars'. Only about six a year are recovered; but over the
aeons of time, a major meteoric catastrophe has
occurred every 50 million years. It is now 65 million
years since the Yucatan catastrophe . . .

Now, one of the pleasures of living by the beach is
that one can take a blanket and a cushion, and lie down
at night on the shingle and simply gaze up at the night
sky. The Milky Way spans the canopy of heaven, which
slowly rotates round the Pole throughout the night.
Tiny satellites creep their way across the constellations.
The shooting stars are thrilling – but their message . . .
what does it say to us? Can this precarious galaxy be
part of a homely universe?

Recent opinion suggests that Jupiter may hold part of

the answer to this question. Following the dramatic explosions observed as the comet 'Schumacher-Levy 9' crashed into its turbulent atmosphere, astronomers have pointed out the importance of having such a large planet (or failed sun) in our immediate surroundings. Adrian Berry, Science Correspondent for the *Daily Telegraph*, outlined this new attitude:

> Our solar system has an enormous cloud of tens of billions of comets of which individual members are continually being deflected towards the Sun – sometimes coming dangerously close to our own world . . . As Professor George Wetherill, an astonomer at the Carnegie Institute of Washington, has put it: 'Without a Jupiter-sized world in our planetary system, collisions with large comets and other dangerous objects like massive asteroids might occur with terrible frequency, not once in about 50 million years as they do at present, but at least once every 100,000 years. This would make it extremely difficult for a civilisation to evolve, and the simple answer is that there might not be one.'
>
> In the 1960s, eminent scientist Freeman Dyson . . . suggested that in looking for life elsewhere in the universe, we should seek stars like the Sun that are emitting infra-red light. This would be because advanced civilisations would decide to dismantle the useless bulk of their Jupiter-sized planets and rearrange this material in a vast ring of new planets round their parent suns in what has been called a Dyson Sphere. This structure, that would accommodate a vastly expanded population, and its industries, would interfere with the outgoing light of their suns, hence their infra-red colour. But Jupiter is no useless

bulk, and our descendants would be ill-advised to
dismantle it to build a Dyson Sphere. We need that
planet intact.[8]

Another example of how things work to our advantage
against all the odds is the amazing way water behaves on
cooling: like other materials, it contracts – that is, until
it freezes. Then instead of shrinking, it expands (as people
who go away in winter without keeping their heating
systems on find out to their cost!). Then, below minus
four degrees, the ice recommences the normal shrinking process. This freezing anomaly means that ice is
lighter than water. We take this for granted, but it is
astonishing that the solid should be lighter than the
liquid. As a result, ice forms a 'blanket' on the water, a
thermal insulation mechanism. The oceans retain some
warmth, and teem with life beneath the polar ice.
Otherwise, planet Earth would long ago have become
one solid frozen lifeless mass.

So, as one lies on the beach, gazing up at the shooting stars, and listening to the night sounds of the sea, the
seabirds and the waders, one has the right to glory in the
wonder of it all, thank God for our solar vacuum cleaner,
which deflects those unwanted, dangerous pieces of
debris, and our icy duvet – and imagine the picture God
used to help Job regain his peace of mind:

> Where were you when I laid the earth's foundation
> . . . while the morning stars sang together and all the
> angels shouted for joy. . . Can you bind the beautiful
> Pleiades? Can you loose the cords of Orion? Can
> you bring forth the constellations in their seasons or
> lead out the Bear with its cubs? Do you know the
> laws of the heavens?
>
> (Job 38.4, 7, 31–33)

But, as we have seen, Isaiah and Jeremiah recognized humanity's alienation long before our modern problems; and much of Jesus' teaching was directed at the spiritual recalcitrance of the people of his day. Francis Thompson portrays our problem as one of estranged faces and 'clay-shuttered doors':

> Does the fish soar to find the ocean,
> The eagle plunge to find the air –
> That we ask of the stars in motion
> If they have rumour of thee there?
>
> Not where the wheeling systems darken,
> And our benumbed conceiving soars! –
> The drift of pinions, would we hearken,
> Beats at our own clay-shuttered doors.
>
> The angels keep their ancient places; –
> Turn but a stone, and start a wing!
> 'Tis ye, 'tis your estrangèd faces,
> That miss the many-splendoured thing.[9]

The real problem is not some scientific issue, but something hidden in the twistedness of the human heart, as Jesus' story of the Prodigal Son shows us:

> There was a man who had two sons. The younger one said to his father, 'Father, give me my share of the estate'. So he divided his property between them ... The younger son got together all he had, set off for a distant country and there squandered his wealth ... The older brother answered his father, 'Look! All these years I have been slaving for you and never disobeyed your orders. Yet you never gave me even a young goat so I could celebrate with my

friends'. . . 'My son,' the father said, 'you are always
with me, and everything I have is yours.'

(Luke 15.12–13, 29, 31).

The father's unconditional love sets the scene. His 'being
there' brings the young son home, but alienates the
older brother. Greed destroys relationships, and thus the
younger son only saw the father as a means to an end.
Pride finds love offensive, and made the older son see in
his father's constant presence something demanding and
oppressive, and it blinded him to his generous inheritance.

Sin and salvation

Why then are we so blind? Is it that we have tasted
despair from early in our lives? Is it that death and suffering and disappointment have disillusioned us with
life, with God, with faith? But which came first, death,
disillusion and despair – or sin? Saint Paul says that sin
came first, and death followed (Romans 5.12). Until we
recognize that sin is the primary problem, the ultimate
disaster, we have still not reached the bottom line in
understanding the human predicament. This is not to
say that death is of no consequence. The Epistle to
Hebrews sees a major part of Jesus' victory in terms of
his defeat of death: 'Since the children have flesh and
blood, Jesus too shared in their humanity so that by
death he might destroy him who holds the power of
death – that is the devil – and free those who all their
lives were held in slavery by their fear of death'
(Hebrews 2.14–15).

If sin is the root of our problem, we need a Saviour
who can deliver us from more even than death and the

fear of death. Sin is an aberration of the self, a moral twist which screws up all we have, all we do and all we are. At the very core of our spirit, we are curved in upon ourselves, and only God can put us right. In this he has done everything we need. Real salvation, while it includes and inspires knowledge and understanding, is nothing less than a saving and transforming personal relationship with God, based on faith in Christ, and experienced in the power of the Holy Spirit. This turns our moral twistedness 'inside-out', so that we can be at home and at one with God, and with one another, just like the younger son, once he had learned his lesson.

It is in this experience of a saving personal relationship that Jesus becomes the way, the truth and the life, back to the Father:

> 'Do not let your heart be troubled. Trust in God, trust also in me. In my Father's house are many rooms; if it were not so, I would have told you. I am going there to prepare a place for you. And if I go and prepare a place for you, I will come back and take you to be with me that you also may be where I am. You know the way to the place where I am going.' Thomas said to him, 'Lord we don't know where you are going, so how can we know the way?' Jesus answered, 'I am the way and the truth and the life. No one comes to the Father except through me. If you really knew me, you would know my Father as well.'
>
> (John 14.1–7).

The word for 'rooms' is the Greek equivalent of 'dwelling', and Jesus' promise exactly fits our concept of a homely creation, with God at the heart of it. What is more, Jesus goes on to raise the idea to an even higher level: 'If anyone loves me, he will obey my teaching. My Father will love him, and we will come to him and make our home with him' (John 14.23).

And in the following chapter, Jesus develops the idea, using the picture of a vine to describe the relationship. Once again, Jesus pictured something common to his listeners' experience, less so for us. However, vines are coming back in fashion, and once were common in East Anglia. St Mary's Church in Westley Waterless, nestling in a farmyard above the old London to Norwich road, must have had a vineyard round it once, in the days when it boasted a priory, and Sir John and Lady de Creke bequeathed it the brasses which have made it famous. It also has an ancient 'graffito' scratched by a brother on the reveal of a south window when he totted up the results of a bumper crop using the latest thing in mathematics, one of the earliest examples of Arabic numerals in England. The '8s' lie lazily on their backs! Imagine the scene: They must have piled their baskets in the little nave, while someone kept a tally on the wall. Jesus said:

I am the true vine and my Father is the gardener. He cuts off every branch in me that bears no fruit, while every branch that bears fruit he trims clean so that it will be even more fruitful. You are already clean because of the word I have spoken to you . . . I am the vine, you are the branches. If a man remains in me and I in him, he will bear much fruit; apart from me you can do nothing . . . If you remain in me and my words remain in you, ask whatever you wish, and it will be given you . . . As the Father has loved me, so have I loved you. Now remain in my love.

(John 15.1–13)

The word for abide is from the same root as that for 'rooms', or dwellings in Chapter 14. So we can re-translate it as: 'If you home in on me, and my words find a home in you . . . home in on my love.' Our 'homing in to God' is as intimate and as productive as the fruitful branch which secures itself to the all-suffusing life of the parental vine, and from it comes a vintage yield.

Dwelling on God

We live our lives too much in haste. The theologian, Kosuke Koyama,[10] with a background of Japanese Buddhism, sensitive to the importance of what goes on at the margins of society, and famous for his vividly pictorial writing, has put his finger on the nub, with the titles of two of his books: *Three Mile-an-Hour God* and *Water-Buffalo Theology*! We need to learn to 'dwell' on the important things of life, for only then do we appreciate their full taste, and develop our true potential.

There is a parameter in mechanics called the 'dwell factor'. If you study, for example, a rapidly spinning wheel with the intermittent flashes of a strobe light, you can adjust the light until the wheel seems to stand still; then you can work out its speed, and other important details. Perhaps we can commandeer the phrase, and apply it to the way we live, the way we say our prayers, sing our hymns, and develop our relationships! We need to adjust the speed of our minds (and bodies) till the blurred truths we hurriedly affirm begin to take on a new dimension. The writer Juan Carlos Ortiz, when a pastor in South America, would sometimes preach on or dwell on a particular subject for several weeks, until everyone began to live out its implications.

We should also note the important role language
plays in our faith: Jesus insists that his words are a key to
success. Words are a most powerful tool for good: 'The
pen is mightier than the sword.' Words can reveal truth
and heal the mind. But words can also be one of the
most subtle weapons of wickedness, hiding the truth,
and dividing the home. Even in church language, where
the welcome God extends should be understood by all,
the words used can so often become a barrier. A revealing
cry from the heart comes in a letter to *The Church Times*
from a Hackney rector:

> We are planning to start a monthly 'family service',
> accessible to all ages, and 'user friendly'. We then run
> up against the fact that we are obliged to use words –
> dear Lord, so many words – which are user-hostile.
> The authorized Eucharistic prayers are the biggest
> problem . . . what troubles me more, riffling through
> the collected works of Michel Foucault, is that these
> prayers are prime examples of what he has taught us
> to see in so many texts of our time: the dangerous
> collusion of knowledge, language and power. For all
> that is half-baked, if not downright gobbledegook,
> in Postmodernism, this much at least we have learned
> from its gurus – that texts by those who know, in the
> language of those who know are instruments of
> control and coercion. Sometimes on Sundays, as I
> obediently say what I am supposed to say, I think I
> hear a great cry (not permitted by General Synod):
> 'Let my people go!'[11]

Language is a major factor in what makes a house a
home. Research has affirmed what we would suspect,
that it makes a great difference to the development of

children if parents spend time talking (even using sign language) with them from their earliest moments. We know that the best way to get through to people of another culture is to talk to them in their 'mother tongue'. It may take time to learn how to do it, but it is truly worth the effort. When the love of our heavenly Father is expressed in the intimacy of our mother tongue, we have ground well laid to counteract the sense of alienation which pervades our world. 'Abba', Father, can regain the power Jesus gave it – abba, with mama, being two sounds that most often mark a baby's earliest attempt at language.

We must remember that home should also be a place where we grow up, and become independent, in the right sense of that ambiguous word. Just as the swallow that makes its nest in the old hide works so hard to fledge her brood, so God has the same purpose to bring us to maturity. God is aiming to do more than wrap us up in the warm bedclothes of pious comfort. He intends to use his love not just as a wall of security, but as the parapet from where we will have to fly free in our own growing faith. The chick must grow, the sheep must learn to live among the wolves, the saved must learn to cope even with the dark night of the soul.

The purpose of all this is twofold: first, to wean us, as the Psalmist puts it (Psalm 131.2), so that we begin to grow more like him through learning to take responsibility, avoiding the danger of being diminished by over-dependence on others (including God) to take all the important decisions; and second, as a result, to deepen our relationship with him, so that our faith is strengthened. God aims to build our faith as strong as steel, for 'This is the victory that has overcome the world, even our faith' (1 John 5.4). There is an important sense in which the lord of the household has left the home, and commanded his retainers to get on with things till he comes back (cf. Luke 19.13).

For further reflection

1. In what ways does the story of the prodigal son and the elder brother (Luke 15.11–32) resemble the story of the Pedlar of Swaffham? Are you like one or other or both of them in any ways? What prayer do you think those two brothers should pray?

2. In what ways do you feel you are 'at home'? How 'homely' do you consider your present address? Do you feel at home 'with yourself'? Are you more at home now than you were in the past? Do you still look forward to one day having an Ideal Home?

3. How has this chapter helped you to feel more at home (a) in the world; (b) in the universe beyond?

4. Jesus is the way, the truth and the life – how does this brings us home to God (John 14.1–6)? Suggest ways for 'dwelling' in God's truth. How could this change the way we pray and worship together?

5
God's poem

---∿∿∿∙◯∙∿∿∿---

The power of language

DOWN ON THE BEACH, February is the cruellest month. One's reserves have been drained, and Spring's renewal is only close enough to be tantalizing. One good day gives way to a chill grey wind, and the feeling of being cheated is hard to resist. All the same, the sounds, if not the feel of Spring are there to hold onto, an embryonic language telling us to believe in what as yet we cannot see. The language of birds, in the dawn chorus, which will soon be gathering to a crescendo as day by day March strides on towards the equinox, prepares them for the activity of Spring. Flowers, too, have a language, expressed in their tapestry of colour, preparing them for Summer fruitfulness – daffodils and bluebells in the gardens, followed by a carpet of mauve sea rocket and delicate yellow-horned poppy on the Scalp. For us, the language of Christian hope prepares us for Easter and new experiences in the love of God.

Meanwhile, the sounds of life rise in volume and variety all around us. The bubbling call of the curlews fills the marshes. The shelducks' cries resound across the ponds. Crested grebes vie for attention in a surge of body language. Bright little robins stake out their territory with boisterous trills. Nightingales will soon compete with each other in a heart-stopping song contest, while nearby roe deer bark in surprise, and the moon delights the bushes and spinneys with silvery magic.

In all of this, recognition is one of our most precious possessions. In the book of Genesis, we read that Adam gave names to all his discoveries. Ever since, we have been building on the insights with which language gifts the mind and guides the soul. It should be no surprise, then, to find that those who are born deaf face great obstacles in the process of learning to think, and therefore the development of mental ability as a whole, and are in fact more handicapped than those born blind. Sight and sound, too, are closely linked, as in the story of someone who described the redness of a rose to a blind man, and got the reply: 'Yes, yes! I see! It's just like a fanfare of trumpets!'

The story of Helen Keller brings out the power of language to develop the mind. Born highly intelligent, but blind and deaf from 19 months through scarlet fever, she ceased to progress and became increasingly frustrated and difficult, until one day her teacher, Annie Sullivan, got her to associate the wetness of water on her hand with the vibrations of the word 'water' in Annie's throat. From then on, her grasp of language grew in leaps and bounds, until her mind's eye clearly saw a world to influence, and a mission to fulfil. She became fluent in German and French, studied Classics and Philosophy, learned to ride and swim, and at 23 wrote her first book, *The Story of My Life*.

For us, too, language is the way in which we see the world. As we learn things and recognize patterns, whether on the material, physical, social or spiritual level, we name them, and so build a language by which we can engage them. The more we learn, the more again we come to see; and as our language develops, so we are able to recognize more truths and facts, in situations that previously meant nothing to us. It was said of the first Olympic gold medal shot-putter to break the 20-metre barrier: 'Dallas Long has muscles in places where most people don't even have places.' In a similar way, language helps us develop specific abilities where previously only latent potential existed.

Of course, language can also be powerfully misleading. There are so many competing voices seeking our attention and calling for our support; so many subtly varying languages, some seductive, others disturbing. All too often people attend to the wrong voices, trust the wrong messages and mistake lies for truths. As a result they set off down paths where dreams turn into nightmares; and they have to reassess their whole outlook in order to save what they can from the wreckage.

Language conveys the religious and moral roots of our cultural outlook, and here it is especially subtle and potentially dangerous, because it is so closely related to what we ourselves become, as it is part of the process by which we come to see the world and our place in it. Like car headlights, language is in this respect something we are scarcely aware of – we are so busy using it to see and evaluate everything else. As a result, it becomes particularly hard to correct or criticize, because in doing so, it feels as if our own essential being has been called into question.

Therefore, we need to learn the healthy principle of being able to remain open to self-criticism, realizing it does not undervalue us as persons, but instead raises the level of our true potential. In the light of our experience, as it unfolds, we need to keep reflecting afresh on our deeply held views. We need to make adjustments and the changes that our experience shows to be necessary, without compromising the foundation truths of our faith. Our on-going moral and spiritual well-being needs this continuing self-appraisal. This process is like living on the fault line of an earthquake zone (for example, the San Andreas fault in California) where two plates of the earth's crust meet and the rocks deep below the surface are put under enormous pressure. Two things can happen: either a continual process of small adjustments accompanied by an endless series of earth tremors; or long periods of quiet, while large forces build up silently, till a major earthquake is unleashed. Californians have learnt to appreciate the value of the former situation in spite of its continual instability. We need a language of life which is reliable, but which has the power to adjust itself without in the process losing the original reliability and truth-centredness from which it grows.

The language of promise

To change the metaphor at this point, we can adopt a picture from the Bible: the rock and the river from the story where Moses struck a desert rock to release a spring of water to quench the people's thirst (Exodus 17.6). We need to build our life on the rock of God's being, and his unshakable truths; but at the same time, we need to be able to adjust our application of those truths to the changing and developing realities of the world we encounter, as we journey together through life.

Marxism is an example of a faulty foundation. It was

not built on 'rock' but was based on a flawed ideology.
For a while it provided a language which promised
much, and for years even seemed comparatively successful – almost to the last moment, when suddenly the
whole edifice collapsed. Christianity has, all too often,
exhibited examples of a second weakness. Rising from
the right foundation, the 'river' that flows out has often
failed to adapt to the features of the landscape, in other
words the cultural dynamics of the society it seeks to
serve. Its tendency to live in the past has often left it out
of touch with the present, and unprepared for the
future. Paul reminds the Corinthians of how we may
have the right foundation but still go astray, because we
can base our life on Christ, but build a house of straw
(1 Corinthians 3.10–15).

At the conclusion to the Sermon on the Mount
(Matthew 7.24–29), Jesus said his teaching was a rock
where we could find the basis for our lives. We still have
to face the storms and floods of life, but our foundation
is stable, and the 'house' of our life will stand. Those who
follow other beliefs are building on the shifting sands
of human opinion and the fashions of the day. Under
pressure, their world is liable to collapse. The letter to
Hebrews sees Jesus as God's final word, the exact representation of his being, in human form (Hebrews 1.1–3).
John calls him the 'Word of God' who was with God
and who was God, and goes on to say that the Word was
made flesh and lived among us. Those who had seen
Jesus had 'seen the Father', so those who heard him had
heard God's voice. People were amazed at his teaching,
for he spoke with authority. 'All spoke well of him and
were amazed at the gracious words that came from his

lips' (Luke 4.22). On one occasion, officials were sent to arrest him; but returned empty-handed, saying, 'No one ever spoke the way this man does' (John 7.46).

Jesus' language was a language of promise. He had come to proclaim the good news of the Kingdom of God. He challenged his hearers to listen to the meaning that lay beneath the words, and pressed them to see beyond the mere material images, saying: 'He that has ears to hear, let him hear!' and adding: 'Consider carefully what you hear . . . with the measure you use, it will be measured to you – and even more. Whoever has will be given more; whoever does not have, even what he has will be taken from him' (Mark 4.23–25).

Jesus prefaced his sayings with the striking phrase 'amen, amen' (translated 'verily, verily', or nowadays: 'in truth I tell you'). This significant opening looks back to a declaration by Isaiah about the 'God of Truth'. The Hebrew for 'God of Truth' is literally 'God Amen' – and Amen means 'surely', being related to 'stand firm', 'truth', and 'faithfulness'. 'Whoever invokes a blessing in the land will do so by the 'God of Truth'; he who takes an oath in the land will swear by the God of truth' (Isaiah 65.16). Isaiah was contrasting God Amen (God of Truth) with the gods of Fortune and Destiny, with whom the people were hurrying to place their bets on the lottery of life, as they 'spread a table for Fortune and fill bowls of mixed wine for Destiny' (Isaiah 65.11). In contrast, trust in the Lord is no lottery, since he is prepared not only to hear his people's prayer, but even to anticipate their cry: 'Before they call I will answer, while they are speaking I will hear' (Isaiah 65.24). As Jesus put it, 'When you pray do not keep on babbling . . . for your Father knows what you need before you ask him. This

is how you should pray: 'Our Father in heaven...'
(Matthew 6.7–9).

Paul, who also uses the language of promise, sees God
as the great Amen:

> For no matter how many promises God has made,
> they are 'Yes' in Christ. And so through him the
> 'Amen' is spoken by us to the glory of God. Now it
> is God who makes both us and you stand firm in
> Christ. He anointed us, and set his seal of ownership
> on us, and put his Spirit in our hearts as a deposit,
> guaranteeing what is to come.
>
> (2 Corinthians 1.20–22)

This wonderful language of promise, however, has a
'government health warning' attached! It we neglect
such a great hope, we do so at our peril. This is the
message of the letter to the Hebrews. Chapter 3, in particular, warns the world that when God's promises are
on offer, we must be ever alert, in case we miss what he
intends. The Israelites long ago were led out by Moses,
under God, towards the promised land. However, most
of them preferred their own corrupt desires, and as a
result refused to believe that God would see them
through the great difficulties that seemed to lie ahead.
They died, never having entered their inheritance. Bishop
Westcott wrote a famous commentary on Hebrews, and
he sums up the tension here with the words 'The prize
is glorious, but the peril is great.' As one who grew up
singing the 'Venite' (Psalm 95) every Sunday in church,
I became very familiar with its change of tone, from its
joyful and welcoming beginning to its rather forbidding
and gloomy ending, and can still recite it by heart: 'O
come let us sing unto the Lord, let us rejoice in the

God of our salvation' (verse 1) ... but changing to
(verses 8–11):

> Today if ye will hear his voice, harden not your
> hearts, as in the provocation and as in the day of
> temptation in the wilderness, when your fathers
> tempted me, proved me and saw my works. Forty
> years long was I grieved with this generation and
> said, 'This is a people that do err in their hearts for
> they have not known my ways', unto whom I swear
> in my wrath that they should not enter into my rest.

Some versions had these rather forbidding words in
brackets, and in time it became usual to sing only the
first seven verses, anyway. The version of the 'Venite'
now used in the Anglican Alternative Service Book for
Morning Prayer has exchanged the last four verses with
a verse from Psalm 96 (although, of course, in the
Psalter, Psalm 95 is given correctly). Surely, I say to
myself, something has been overlooked – and, indeed,
I personally overlooked it in my youth. Nowadays, I
believe those last four verses are actually the most exciting part of the Psalm! The seemingly dire warning is in
fact an expression of supreme elation. The Psalmist is
crying out 'Come on, take your fill of God's overflowing
generosity! Bring out your buckets, your watering cans,
your open groundsheets. Spread every receptacle that
can hold blessing out before the Lord! Empty out the
flowers from your decorative vases, take the lid off your
coffee pots and tea pots, your urns and your jugs. Don't
miss out on a single drop of the unspeakably wonderful
gifts of love and blessing God is longing to pour out
upon you.' The gloomy ending of the 'Venite' needs to
be sung in a positive spirit with vivid imagination.

Nothing less will prepare the congregation for the wonderful feast of good things which lies ahead of them in the liturgy and all it represents. Such is the true force of the language of promise, when a people learn to talk and think that way.

God's promise is that we should not only hear about him, but become like him. God's words give us a vision of God, and our vision of God transforms our lives, for: 'We know that when he appears, we shall be like him, for we shall see him as he is. Everyone who has this hope in him purifies himself, just as he is pure' (1 John 3.2–3). John is building here on what Jesus said in the Beatitudes: 'Blessed are the pure in heart, for they shall see God' (Matthew 5.8). Purity itself is a gift which comes to us through the language of promise, which empowers us to escape the forces of moral corruption: 'God . . . has given us very great and precious promises, so that through them you may participate in the divine nature and escape the corruption in the world caused by evil desires' (2 Peter 1.3–4). The promise to those who believe is that God dwells in them by his Holy Spirit, enabling them to participate in the new nature he gives and to share as his children the family likeness of purity and holiness.

However, Peter goes on to warn us that if we fail to live out these truths, we will become 'near-sighted and blind' and will soon forget that we have been cleansed from our past sins (2 Peter 1.5–9). Peter, whose time is short, says he will keep reminding them of these things 'even though you already know them', and will write them down for the benefit of future generations (2 Peter 1.12–15). So memory, too, plays an important part in the process. We too should activate the powers of our memories, by re-reading and, indeed, retelling the promises on which our faith depends, continually focusing our lives upon them. Both for Jews, under the old covenant, and Christians, under the new, remembering God's promises and actions collectively has always been an important part of the life of a believing community. At Passover, the youngest member of a Jewish family asks, 'What does this ceremony mean to you?' At the Holy Communion, we share the simple feast of bread and wine 'in remembrance' of Christ. We all know from experience that what is taught and supposedly learnt on a single occasion is often quickly forgotten. Any teacher ignores that to their cost. Any pupil knows that many sessions of revision are necessary to master a subject. We have little difficulty in remembering things which form the daily pattern of our lives. The strength of words is only seen when they are heard, understood, acted upon and frequently recalled. This is a vital element in our progress to spiritual maturity.

Language, then, is a fundamental factor in how we receive our personal share in the divine nature. God's vivid truth must be imprinted onto our common life, just as the law God gave to Moses was imprinted on tablets of stone. Now, our transformed hearts and lives should carry a message that everyone can read, just as Paul said to his friends at Corinth, 'You show that you are a letter from Christ, the result of our ministry, written not with ink but with the Spirit of the living God, not on tablets of stone but on tablets of human hearts' (2 Corinthians 3.2–3). Ink may fade or be erased, but the Spirit of God builds through our lives a language of love and reconciliation, of joy in sorrow, riches in poverty, of patience, kindness, purity, understanding and truthful speech (2 Corinthians 6.4–10). This becomes the message of the Gospel for those around us, a memorable language, spoken, understood and recollected, and now re-embodied, as we in our turn represent Christ, God's Word, to mankind.

The language of science

As Christians who believe it is important to recognize God at the centre of everything, we need to come to terms with the language of science, since some people see it as a language which has taken over from faith. The language of science is ultimately mathematical (which is the best form for expressing very exact physical, and in some cases logical, relationships). It also employs words and concepts which have become part of everyday use, like gravity, electron and quantum. These words are technical terms which describe what happens in certain physical situations. In order to see why this language in its present form is now complementary to the language of faith, we shall look very briefly at how it has developed through three stages: dealing, originally, with the question 'why' certain things happen in nature (and often giving an important place to God); moving on to 'how' these things happen (where exact observation takes over from theory – while God and his angels are only brought in to fill the missing links); and finally, in our own era, dealing only with 'what' is going on – while 'how' it ultimately happens (let alone 'why') is seen to be unknowable. Of course, knowing 'what happens' is very important, even if it leaves out 'why' and 'how'. As the scientific writer Bruce Gregory puts it: 'No matter how firmly someone believes he can fly simply by flaying his arms, it is unwise for him to step off the roof of a tall building. No matter how convinced a Buddhist is that the world is an illusion, she invariably leaves a room by walking through the doorway rather than through a wall.'[1]

Aristotle (384–322 BC) set the scene, with a language which held sway for centuries. In broad terms, the question being asked at that period was 'Why?' Why does fire rise upwards, while rocks fall downwards? Because upwards is heavenly, a place of unchanging essence, while downwards is towards changeability and decay. Ptolemy in the second century AD outlined a view of the universe from this perspective, partly to help people understand how the stars were supposed to influence their lives. For example, because they believed everything in the heavens had to be perfect, everything, with earth in the centre, had to move in circles, as any other shape would be 'imperfect'. The irregular movements of the planets (due to their actually moving round the sun) had to be accounted for by adding extra circles, or 'epicycles' to their supposed trajectory.

In the early sixteenth century, Copernicus (1473–1543) broke the mould, and decided that the sun must be at the centre, with earth revolving round it. Kepler (1571–1630), in the seventeeth century, broke another taboo, showing that the planets did not move in circles, but in ellipses (but he thought angels might have a part to play in making this unprecedented form of motion possible!); and soon after, Galileo (1564–1642) articulated what would become the guiding metaphor of physical science: 'The Universe, which stands continually open to our gaze, cannot be understood unless one first learns to comprehend the language and read the letters in which it is composed. It is written in the language of mathematics.[2] From then on, the central scientific question was not 'why?', but 'how?': how much? how far? how long? – no matter if the results did not fit our preconceptions of what 'ought to be'.

Sir Isaac Newton (1642–1727) firmly established the new language of science with a set of all-embracing formulae. Now, it seemed that nature was a vast, but ultimately simple, piece of machinery – though what held it all together remained mysterious. While Newton had no doubt that God was involved, his mathematical equations assumed the existence of a mysterious factor – 'gravity'. When he was asked how 'gravity' worked, he simply replied, 'I do not make hypotheses.' Gravity became a familiar part of the language, though its nature remained wholly mysterious. Its value lay in its mathematics. In the meantime, 'God' was quietly edged out from the central stage in the language of science.

The poet Alexander Pope (1688–1744) summed up the elation of those days in a couplet which is thoroughly approving:

> Nature and Nature's laws lay hid in night:
> God said, Let Newton be! and all was light.[3]

Nevertheless, the new agnosticism about how reality worked troubled philosophers like David Hume (1711–1776) and Immanuel Kant (1724–1804), who tried to provide a reliable 'rock' on which to base the rapidly growing and increasingly successful 'scientific enterprise'. Kant's *Critique of Pure Reason* was the basis which won the day, but it left human reason dangerously autonomous in a world of mysterious essences (or 'noumena', as he called the unknowable principles which are somehow

behind the world we experience). Poets, too, felt uneasy
about the consequences of what was happening: William
Wordsworth (1770–1850) was horrified at the way the
new science seemed bent on explaining away the wonder
of life:

> Sweet is the lore which Nature brings;
> Our meddling intellect
> Mis-shapes the beauteous form of things:
> We murder to dissect.
> Enough of Science . . .[4]

However, on contemplating a bust of Newton, Wordsworth found it to be:

> The marble index of a mind forever
> Voyaging through strange seas of thought, alone.[5]

William Blake was even more critical:

> . . . May God us keep
> From Single vision & Newton's Sleep![6]

In our own century, Albert Einstein (1879–1955), who
spent years pondering how light 'worked', extended
Newton's language (now called the language of classical
physics) and showed that light, energy and matter are
ultimately interchangeable. The power of this extended
language of 'special relativity' has been demonstrated by
the development of nuclear energy, for good or ill. His
'general relativity' went further, linking time and space
as part of the way in which gravity 'works'. However, a
new age was dawning, and all the old seeming certainties
of classical physics, even with Einstein's extensions, were
about to go into the melting pot. It was very hard to

accept. As Wittgenstein said, 'A picture held us captive. And we could not get outside of it, for it lay in our language, and language seemed to repeat it to us inexorably.'[7]

Einstein himself never accepted this new revolutionary language – the language of 'quantum mechanics'. Nevertheless, it has been generally accepted as the right language to carry science forward, at least at the subatomic level, where Newton's laws no longer work. The language of quantum mechanics presents ultimate reality as unpredictable, although this 'uncertainty principle' is balanced in practice by a powerful language of prediction which uses mathematical laws of 'probability'.

So, just as 'why?' gave way to 'how?', 'how?' itself has given way to 'what?' At the quantum level we can, it seems, never know how things happen; we can only describe and learn to predict what goes on. The Danish physicist Niels Bohr (1885–1962) worked out how to describe what is going on when radiation occurs through the movement of electrons. This led on to the language of 'complementarity', where the electron is treated both as a moving particle and as a stationary wave. He said, 'There is no quantum world. There is only an abstract quantum physical description. It is wrong to think that the task of physics is to find out how nature is. Physics concerns only what we can say about nature.'[8]

The physicist Richard Feynman (1918–1993) worked out a different way to describe what was happening. It involved diagrams which even treated certain events as moving backwards as well as forwards in time. The results agreed with previous formulae, but could be used to measure events much more accurately. At first, Bohr treated Feynman's diagrams as pictures, and was convinced as a result that Feynman did not understand quantum mechanics. He failed to grasp that the diagrams are not pictures of how things work, but were what Feynman called book-keeping devices. Feynman pointed out the impossibility of probing beneath the surface of events, so as to picture what is really going on, writing that:

> There was a time when the newspapers said that only twelve men understood the theory of relativity. I do not believe there ever was such a time. There might have been a time when only one man did, because he was the only guy who caught on, before he wrote his paper. But after people read the paper a lot of people understood the theory of relativity in some way or other, certainly more than twelve. On the other hand, I think I can safely say that no one understands quantum mechanics ... Do not keep saying to yourself, if you possibly can avoid it, 'But how can it be like that?' because you will get 'down the drain', into a blind alley from which nobody has yet escaped. Nobody knows how it can be like that.[9]

And Bohr said much the same: 'If anybody says he can think about quantum problems without getting giddy, that only shows he has not understood the first thing about them.'

In recent years, science, once the focus of almost universal admiration, is having to learn to meet a growing mood of disenchantment. There has been a trend in some quarters to criticize its methods and results. Friedrich Nietzsche, the nineteenth-century German philosopher, foretold that this would happen, once the religious basis of European culture had been undermined. Famous for the phrase 'God is dead', he personally accepted the trend to atheism, but viewed its outcome with despair, expecting an eclipse of moral values. He prophesied that Christianity, whose single-minded dedication to truth had been a major factor in the rise of science, would eventually undermine itself, as its own tenets were shown to be scientifically groundless.

The author Tom Wolfe outlined the state of play as he saw it, in a recent article, where he says:

Nietzsche predicted that eventually modern science would turn its juggernaut of scepticism upon itself, question the validity of its own foundations, tear them apart, and self-destruct. The scorn the new breed heaps upon quantum mechanics ('has no real-world applications'. . . 'depends entirely on fairies sprinkling goofball equations in your eyes') . . . has become withering. If only Nietzsche were alive! He would have relished every minute of it!

Recently I happened to be talking to a prominent Californian geologist, and she told me: 'When I first went into geology, we all thought that in science you create a solid layer of findings, through experiment and careful investigation, and then you add a second layer, like a second layer of bricks, all very carefully, and so on . . . but we now realize that the very first layers aren't even resting on solid ground. They are balanced on bubbles, on concepts that are full of air, and those bubbles are being burst today, one after the other.'

I suddenly had a picture of the entire astonishing edifice collapsing and modern man plunging headlong back into the primordial ooze. He's floundering, sloshing about, gulping for air, frantically treading ooze, when he feels something huge and smooth swim beneath him and boost him up, like some almighty dolphin. He can't see it, but he's much impressed. He names it God.'[10]

The scientific enterprise will continue to lose credibility if its achievements are put to selfish, inhumane and unnatural uses. The answer to bad science is not the abolition of science, but the pursuit of better science, and in particular, the doing of it in ways which acknowledge God at the centre of it all. This involves at least two characteristics which have alsways been the hallmark of Christian intellectual endeavour. The first one is a 'dedicated Christian mind', which has been defined as: 'A mind trained, informed, equipped to handle data of secular controversy within a framework of reference which is constructed of Christian presuppositions'.[11]

The second characteristic is an attitude of gratitude and obedience towards a just and loving infinite, personal, Creator, such that:

> In the place of the craven fear instilled by a pagan theology of nature – the fear of being regarded as an unwelcome and over-inquisitive intruder in matters that are not his business – the Christian who finds scientific talents in his tool bag has quite a different fear – the fear that his Father should judge him guilty of neglecting his stewardly responsibilities by failing to pursue the opportunities for good that may be opened up by the new developments.[12]

As I occasionally lie out at night on the beach, and gaze at the stars, I do not fear what may happen from that quarter, for this is to me a homely universe. However, I am troubled about what human beings can do to this world by misusing the tremendous power which science has put at our disposal. So, if the flood-warning siren sounds, warning of a surge in the North Sea, I will try to take adequate precautions; but if global warming causes the oceans to rise so that our bungalow (or far more seriously, the country of Bangladesh, which gave us the word 'bungalow') is submerged, then I will blame those who refused to heed the scientific studies which demonstrate that global warming 'carries a human fingerprint'. Those who, for vested interests, choose to denigrate science when it tells us to restrict pollution and ecological exploitation, are doing no one a service; and those who undermine science as a rational language in the name of some 'freer' alternative, are equally preparing the stage for a world where, as Jesus put it, 'the blind lead the blind, so that both will fall into the ditch' (Matthew 15.14).

In the final analysis, each of us has a choice between retaining our personal independence in the name of our right to 'autonomous selfhood' and surrendering that right to God, so as to bow to his sovereign will and receive his gift of salvation. It is in the pursuit of this second option that we shall conclude our thoughts, by exploring the new language of liberation through surrender which God inspires within us, and thinking about the 'poem' he composes through the language of our lives.

A new language

This new language is, as it should be, based on rock, and begins by a rock, in Lebanon at Banias, where water wells up to become a primary source of the River Jordan.

Banias is the modern name for Caesareia Philippi – where Jesus asked his disciples: 'Who do you say I am?' (Matthew 16.15). Peter's 'You are the Christ' became the rock on which Jesus built his church. This was a watershed point in Jesus' life, and from then on he began to teach them how different his 'Messiahship' must be, compared to popular expectations. There would be no 'long march' to raise a revolutionary army, confront the powers of Rome, and liberate the nation . . . Instead, Jesus would offer himself up to be arrested, judged and put to death – and then to 'rise again'.

As we saw earlier, Jesus' life-work was always leading to the cross. It would be there, in contrast to the Devil's suggestion, that being 'lifted up', he would draw all people to himself, and guarantee the eternal security of all who come. St Paul sums up the implications for us, in terms of a new confidence and wonder:

> If God is for us, who can be against us? He who did not spare his own Son, but gave him up for us all – how will he not also, along with him, graciously give us all things? . . . Christ Jesus who died – more than that, who was raised to life – is at the right hand of God and is also interceding for us. Who shall separate us from the love of Christ . . .? I am convinced that neither death nor life, neither angels nor demons, neither the present nor the future, nor any power, neither height nor depth, nor anything else in all creation, will be able to separate us from the love of God that is in Christ Jesus our Lord.
>
> (Romans 8.31–39)

From the Good Friday Event springs the language of love, justice, wonder and transformation. It is a language which encompasses everything, since by putting God at the centre of everything, and relating his victorious power and love to the very heart of darkness, we can know that all things may be redeemed. Only that spirit of autonomous selfhood, which wantonly rejects God's grace, can have by definition, as it were, no place in this great scheme of things.

Let me use the story of the Hubble telescope to illustrate the way the cross envisions us. This telescope was placed in orbit to survey the deepest fields of space, probing back in time to the origins of the universe. To begin with, by a drastic oversight, its great mirror was a hair's breadth out of true. As a result, its vision was blurred. In 1993 a mission was launched to replace parts of the optical apparatus, under Colonel Storey Musgrave. The brilliant operation was performed with astonishing success. Musgrave himself carried out the final exercise, to replace a magnetometer near the top. Having completed the task, he says, he took the opportunity to climb a few steps to the very top. As he turned his head, he saw the world below him, breathtaking in all its colouration and vitality. That sight was the supreme moment of his life. It seemed so close and so colossal, he felt he could just reach out and touch it. At Houston, they too saw the scene, through his video-camera, and he heard a voice gasp in amazement: 'The view, Storey, the view!'

There is a sense in which that telescope gives us a parable of the cross for this our day and age. Just as Hubble began as an out-of-focus vision of the universe, so our vision of life has been blurred and mistaken in so many ways. However, in what happened on the cross, our ultimate vision, too, may be renewed.

Just as Hubble's scientific optics can reach back towards the start of time, so through the cross our spiritual vision can discern the eternal being of the God of love, and we are filled with wonder and worship for him. For in Jesus, lifted up, we see God's true nature revealed in a way that speaks our language, in a human form which relates totally to our condition. We also see what Peter calls the Lamb prepared before the foundation of the world, the one who was ready to pay the price of creating a human race who had the gift of freedom, and might choose evil instead of good.

And as from Hubble, Musgrave looked down on earth, so from the cross, we see how God perceives humanity, as something beautiful and precious, and worth in every way the infinite cost to himself which was involved in our redemption, and at the same time, in the person of the human Jesus, we see what humanity can become when it returns to walk faithfully in perfect obedience to the will of God.

So that is it . . . God's purpose is to let us see himself, so that we may become like him in glory. People have often felt uncomfortable with the idea that God made us to glorify himself; and yet that is exactly his amazing plan. However, God does not need our worship, he is not incomplete in himself and dependent for self-fulfilment on worshippers who will return his love. 'God is love' (1 John 4.16), but as the truth of the Trinity makes clear, that love is already fulfilled perfectly in the relationship that eternally exists between Father, Son and Spirit. It is that Triune being who said, 'Let us make man in our own image', and made us male and female, so that with God, we are a threefold entity – 'A cord of three strands is not quickly broken' (Ecclesiastes 4.12).

Paul's letter to the Ephesians

Paul sums up the outcome of all these issues in the letter
to Ephesians. In Chapter 1, he tells of how God planned
the whole process in eternity. In Chapter 2, he outlines
how God has picked us up out of the gutter of life, dead
as we were in trespasses and sins, to bring us to life
through Christ. From this unlikely material, God has set
out to compose a 'poem' (Chapter 2.10 – usually translated 'workmanship', but the Greek word is 'poem').

In Chapter 3, Paul describes how that 'poem' is God's
way of telling all the powers of the universe about the
wonders of his love. Paul uses a word to fit the occasion,
polypoikilos – often used of a beautiful tapestry, or a
glorious flower arrangement. It tells of a harmony of
colour, texture and designs, of many parts all drawn
together, and resplendent, living proof of God's wisdom,
love and power: 'God's intent was that now, through the
church, the manifold [*polypoikilos*] wisdom of God should
be made known to the rulers and authorities in the
heavenly realms' (Ephesians 3.10). What has made such
an unheard-of unity, harmony and beauty possible in
the torn and tragic situation of humanity?

The breakthrough, says Paul, is what happened on the
cross, and

> now in Christ Jesus you who once were far away
> have been brought near through the blood of Christ.
> For he himself is our peace, who has made the two
> one and has destroyed the barrier, the dividing wall
> of hostility... His purpose was to create in himself
> one new man out of the two, thus making peace, and
> in one body to reconcile both of them to God
> through the cross, by which he put to death their

hostility. He came and preached peace to you who
were far away and peace to those who were near. For
through him we both have access to the Father by
one Spirit . . . You are members of God's household,
built on the foundation of the apostles and prophets,
with Christ Jesus himself as the chief cornerstone.
In him the whole building is joined together and
rises to become a holy temple in the Lord. And in
him you too are being built together to become a
dwelling in which God lives by his Spirit.

(Ephesians 2.13–22)

Chapter 4 takes up this theme, calling for each one of us
to draw together, affirm each other, learn from each
other, and grow up with 'that which every part supplies'
into nothing less than the fullness of Christ, through
the spiritual power and resources which the Holy Spirit
makes available to all of us.

And how may we respond to this great vision? How
may we unite, be built together, so as to be crafted by
God into his poetic masterpiece, in a way which will
clearly reveal God to all? How may this transformational
language become our very mother tongue? Paul has
ultimately but one answer, and, as Abraham Lincoln said
of himself, when he has nowhere else to go, he goes
down on his knees. Prayer is above all where we learn
to speak this language. Prayer is above all where we
'learn to see'. On our knees we can see further than
from a mountain top, or even the Hubble telescope. For
as someone said, prayer is not an elastic band, something
to twang from time to time. Prayer is like a muscle,
which grows with use, develops with insight, and in
time it gives us 'muscles in places where most people
don't even have places'.

Prayer is the place where we are brought together on common ground, kneeling before God and reconciled to him and one another through the cross. As we open ourselves to God's riches, we can start to catch the great vision together of God's purposes for the world. From our many different backgrounds and viewpoints can be woven that unity of purpose and power which Jesus promised would bring his special presence (Matthew 18.19–20). As we dwell in this presence we learn to understand his ways and are drawn into his purposes. The language of prayer will become the familiar way by which we face daily life and bigger events. Prayer challenges us to see things as God sees them, and to ask in faith for those things for which as yet there is no evidence. As we see him act in answer to our prayers, our faith should grow, as we see further and become bolder. It enables us to earth God's riches and resources in our needy world, and expect the transformation which his love can bring.

So Paul, in Ephesians 3.14–21, tells us that he kneels before the Father and says:

> I pray that out of his glorious riches he may strengthen you with power through his Spirit in your inner being, so that Christ may dwell in your hearts through faith. And I pray that you, being rooted and established in love, may have power, together with all the saints, to grasp how wide and long and high and deep is the love of Christ, and to know this love that surpasses knowledge – that you may be filled to the measure of all the fullness of God. Now to him who is able to do immeasurably more than all we ask or imagine, according to his power that is at work within us, to him be glory in the church and in Christ

Jesus throughout all generations, for ever and ever!
Amen.

What a poem, what a view!

For further reflection

1. Look at a bank note! Find the promise printed
   on it. Spend some moments thinking about
   how valuable that promise could be to you.
   What could it mean in your life? Compose a
   prayer in the light of your thoughts and feelings.
2. This chapter uses the word 'language' in a com-
   prehensive sense, as in 'the language of promise,
   the language of science'. What language do you
   feel your life speaks? How far does it speak the
   language of promise or of hope? Do you ever
   feel pressured by the world around you to speak
   the language of despair, or of materialism, or of
   prejudice?
3. If you belong to a church, what do you think
   your church and fellowship is 'saying' to the wider
   community by its existence, programme and
   way its members go about their lives? Have you
   ever tried to find out? How could you do so?
4. How has this chapter helped you see God? How
   might understanding about the trend in science
   from 'why?' to 'how?' and then to 'what?' make
   it clearer that science and faith complement
   each other?
5. Pray Paul's prayer (Ephesians 3.14–21), first of
   all changing 'you' to 'me'. Pray it again, using
   the name of someone you choose in place of
   'you'.

Postscript

————•◦◦•————

DOWN BY THE BEACH, Easter can be spring idealized. The sun has some strength at last, the ponds on the reserve reflect the blue sky. New birds are constantly arriving, while the ducks are pairing off. But there can be another factor: the wind! Keep off the beach if the strength of the wind upsets you. There is nowhere to hide (except indoors). Otherwise, let's make the most of it! The sailing club is re-opening, and a forest of masts starts to appear. Soon a host of billowing sails will be spread to catch the wind, hoisted by streamlined Lasers, strong and steady Enterprises, powerful Fireballs, bounding Darts (catamarans) and sail-boarding wind-surfers, ranging from beginners for whom the wind is a disaster, to those experts for whom wind, water, sail, board and body form one pliant, leaping whole.

Far simpler, and more reflective, is kite-flying. With a couple of aerofoil kites, banked one above the other, a string in each hand, and, in one's imagination, up there with the kite sensing land, air and water with the sharp eyes and instant reflexes of a bird of prey – then the fun begins. With a kite you can fly; swoop so fiercely that the spectators scatter; spiral back up, float on the wind, gaze far and wide across sea, marsh, sand and field; bank, twist, pounce and spin – only the arctic gyrfalcon can match a display of this sort! With a little more wind, the kite and its handler really do begin to attain lift-off,

117

defying gravity like some moon-walking astronaut, over
the shingle.

If you can fly a kite this way, you can learn to live and
relish the power of the Easter experience, and the exhil-
aration of the Spirit of Pentecost. This discovery is for
everyone. If it is recognized at the periphery of life, it
must be carried to the centre. Easter people must be
dawn people, so that wherever we go, we see everything
lit up by the brightness of Christ's risen glory, shining
out of the darkness of the cross. If at times a battle has
to be fought between light and darkness, the light must
find its strength in the joy which faith and imagination
can inspire. 'Let us fix our eyes on Jesus, the author and
perfecter of our faith, who for the joy set before him
endured the cross, scorning the shame, and sat down at
the right hand of the throne of God. Consider him who
endured such opposition from sinful men, so that you
will not grow weary and lose heart' (Hebrews 12.2–3).

Notes

All Bible references are taken from the New International Version, copyright © 1973, 1978, 1984 by International Bible Society. Used by permission.

INTRODUCTION

1. *The Oxford Dictionary of Quotations*, Oxford University Press, Oxford, 1953, from *Brewster's Memoirs of Newton*, vol. ii, Chapter 27.
2. David F. Ford (ed.) *The Modern Theologians*, vol. 2, Blackwell, Oxford, 1989, p. 227.
3. Kosuke Koyama, *Mount Fuji and Mount Sinai: A Pilgrimage in Theology*, SCM Press, London, 1984, pp. 15–16.

CHAPTER 1: *Nisi Dominus*

1. John Bingham, *Salute to a Village*, Snettisham Parish Council, 1989.
2. V. R. W. Trowbridge, *Queen Alexandra*, T. Fisher Unwin Ltd, London, 1921, p.54.
3. Robert Hardy, *A Tour of Snettisham*, privately duplicated, 1987.
4. Virgil, *Georgics*, vol. 2, books 3–4, (book 4, lines 212–15), Cambridge Greek and Latin Classics, Cambridge University Press, Cambridge, 1988.
5. W. B. Yeats, *The Second Coming*, Faber Book of Modern Verse, Faber and Faber, London, 1960.
6. Sister Mary Magdalene, *Jesus, Man of Prayer*, The Jesus Library, Hodder and Stoughton, London, 1987.
7. R. A. Finlayson entry: 'God', *New Bible Dictionary*, IVP, Leicester, 1982.
8. Gerard Manley Hopkins, 'God's Grandeur', *The New Oxford Book of English Verse*, Oxford University Press, Oxford, 1972, p. 786.

9. F. L. Hosmer, 'Thy kingdom come! On bended knee', *Hymns Ancient and Modern*, no. 178, Hymns Ancient and Modern Ltd, Norwich, 1983.

CHAPTER 2: *Wash and flood*

1. Graham Swift, *Waterland*, Pan Books Ltd, London, 1984.
2. B. Calgrave, *Felix's Life of St. Guthlac*, tr., Cambridge University Press, Cambridge, 1955.
3. Edward Storey, *Fen, Fire and Flood*, Cambridgeshire Libraries Publications, Peterborough, undated, p. 14.
4. Arthur Codd, BBC Radio 4, *On This Day: The News of Fifty Years Ago,* 18 February 1997.
5. Philip Smith, BBC Radio 4, *On This Day: The News of Fifty Years Ago,* 18 February 1997.
6. Matthew Arnold, 'Dover Beach', *The New Oxford Book of English Verse*, Oxford University Press, Oxford, 1972, p. 703.
7. John Drane, *What is the New Age Saying to the Church?*, Marshall Pickering, London, 1991. See also John Drane, *Faith in a Changing Culture*, Marshall Pickering, London, 1997.
8. Gerard Manley Hopkins, 'God's Grandeur', *The New Oxford Book of English Verse*, Oxford University Press, Oxford, 1972, p. 786.
9. Philip Larkin, 'Church Going', 2 July 1954, *The Less Deceived*, The Marvell Press, 5 Los Angeles Court, St Kilda East, Victoria 3183, Australia, p. 28.
10. Philip Larkin, 'Water', 6 April 1954, *The Whitsun Weddings*, Faber and Faber, London, 1964.
11. John Seymour, *Companion Guide to East Anglia*, Collins, London 1970, p. 208.
12. Margaret Gallyon, *Margery Kempe of Lynn and Medieval England*, The Canterbury Press, Norwich, 1995. See also B. A. Windeatt, *The Book of Margery Kempe*, Penguin, London, 1994.

CHAPTER 3: *Wisdom in the wilderness*

1. *Ardnamurchan: Annals of the Parish*, 2nd edn 1990, Editor, c/o The Post Office, Kilchoan, Argyll, PH36. See also *The Poetry of Scotland*, ed. Roderick Watson, Edinburgh University Press, Edinburgh, 1995, p.263.

2. John Keats, 'La Belle Dame Sans Merci', *Oxford Book of English Verse*, Clarendon Press, Oxford, 1925.

3. Bruce Robinson, *Norfolk Mysteries Revisited*, Elmstead Publications, Wicklewood, Norfolk, NR18 9QL, 1996.

4. Francis Proctor and Philippa Miller, *Village Signs in Norfolk*, vol. 1, Black Horse Press, 8 & 10 Wensum Street, Norwich, NR3 1HR, 1973, p. 81.

5. Fyodor Dostoevsky, *The Brothers Karamazov*, tr. with introduction and notes by Ignat Avsey, Oxford University Press, Oxford, 1994.

6. Ruari Maclean, 'Obituary', *The Independent*, 29 June 1992, p. 14.

7. Katherine A. M. Kelly, 'Give me a Sight, O Saviour', *Mission Praise*, Marshall Morgan and Scott, 1983, words © National Young Life Campaign, Spring Cottage, Spring Road, Leeds, LS6 1AD.

CHAPTER 4: *Homing in*

1, *The Alternative Service Book*, Published by William Clowes, London, SPCK, London, and Cambridge University Press, Cambridge, 1980, §2, p. 144.

2. Mother Teresa, in *Tapestry of Voices*, ed. Michelle Guinness, Triangle, SPCK, 1993.

3. William Wordsworth, 'Intimations of Immortality from Recollections of Early Childhood', *The New Oxford Book of English Verse*, Oxford University Press, Oxford, 1972.

4. Blaise Pascal, *Pensées*, No. 392, J. M. Dent, London, 1973.

5. Blaise Pascal, *Pensées*, No. 217, J. M. Dent, London, 1973.

6. Russell Stannard, *Our Universe*, Kingfisher Larousse, London, 1995, p. 83.

7. *The Times*, Thursday, 2 July 1908, letter to the editor. See also John S. Lewis, *Rain of Iron and Ice*, Helix Editions, Oxford, 1995.

8. Adrian Berry, science correspondent, *Daily Telegraph*, Saturday Profile article, February 1996.

9. Francis Thompson, 'In No Strange Land', *The New Oxford Book of English Verse*, Oxford University Press, Oxford, 1972.

10. David F. Ford (ed.), *The Modern Theologians*, vol. 2, Blackwell, Oxford, 1989, pp. 225–9.

11. John Pridmore, Diary, *The Church Times*, 14 February 1997.

CHAPTER 5: *God's poem*

1. Bruce Gregory, *Inventing Reality: Physics as Language*, Wiley Science Editions, John Wiley & Sons. Inc., New York, 1988.
2. Galilei Galileo, *Discoveries and Opinions of Galileo*, tr., with introduction and notes by S. Drake, Anchor Original, Doubleday, Garden City, NY, 1957, quoted in Gregory, *Inventing Reality*.
3. Alexander Pope, 'Epitaph Intended for Sir Isaac Newton', in Westminster Abbey', *Selected Poetry*, Oxford University Press, Oxford, 1996.
4. William Wordsworth, 'The Tables Turned – An Evening upon the Same Subject', quoted in Gregory, *Inventing Reality*.
5. William Wordsworth, *The Prelude*, Book 3, ed. J. C. Maxwell, Penguin, Harmondsworth, 1971, lines 61–2, quoted in Gregory, *Inventing Reality*.
6. William Blake, 'Letter to Thomas Butt', 22 November 1822, *Letters of William Blake*, ed. Geoffrey Keynes, Rupert Hart-Davis, London, 1956, p. 75.
7. Ludwig Wittgenstein, *Philosophical Investigations*, tr. G. Anscombe, Macmillan, New York, 1958, p. 48.
8. Niels Bohr, *Niels Bohr: A Centenary Volume*, 1985, quoted in Gregory, *Inventing Reality*.
9. Richard Feynman, *The Character of Physical Law*, 1967, quoted in Gregory, *Inventing Reality*.
10. Tom Wolfe, 'Sorry, But Your Soul Just Died', *Independent on Sunday*, 2 February 1997.
11. Henry Blamires, *The Christian Mind*, SPCK, London, 1963, p. 70.
12. Donald M. McKay, *The Open Mind*, IVP, Leicester, 1988, p. 102.